What Happens When Husbands and Wives Pray Together?

**Carey Moore
and Pamela Rosewell Moore**

Foreword by Ruth Bell Graham

SPIRE

© 1992 by Carey Moore and Pamela Rosewell Moore

Published by Fleming H. Revell
a division of Baker Book House Company
P.O. Box 6287, Grand Rapids, MI 49516-6287

Spire edition published 1999

Previously published under the title *If Two Shall Agree: Praying Together as a Couple*

Third printing, January 2000

Printed in the United States of America

ISBN 0-8007-8659-9

The names of some persons mentioned in this book have been changed to protect their privacy.

Material on pages 164–65 is from *Love for a Lifetime* by Dr. James C. Dobson, copyright © 1987 by James C. Dobson. Published by Multnomah Press, Portland, Oregon 97266. Used by permission.

Material on pages 147, 149 is from *Toward Jerusalem* by Amy Carmichael. The Christian Literature Crusade, Fort Washington, Pennsylvania. Used by permission.

Unless otherwise indicated, Scripture quotations are from the HOLY BIBLE, NEW INTERNATIONAL VERSION®. NIV®. Copyright © 1973, 1978, 1984 by International Bible Society. Used by permission of Zondervan Publishing House. All rights reserved.

Scripture quotations identified KJV are from the King James Version of the Bible.

Scripture quotations identified NASB are from the NEW AMERICAN STANDARD BIBLE ®. Copyright © The Lockman Foundation 1960, 1962, 1963, 1968, 1971, 1972, 1973, 1975, 1977. Used by permission.

Scripture quotations identified NEB are from *The New English Bible.* Copyright © 1961, 1970, 1989 by The Delegates of Oxford University Press and The Syndics of the Cambridge University Press. Reprinted by permission.

Scripture quotations identified TEV are from the Good News Bible. Old Testament copyright © American Bible Society 1976. New Testament copyright © American Bible Society 1966, 1971, 1976. Used by permission.

Scripture quotations identified TLB are from *The Living Bible* © 1971. Used by permission of Tyndale House Publishers, Inc., Wheaton, IL 60189. All rights reserved.

For current information about all releases from Baker Book House, visit our web site:
http://www.bakerbooks.com

We can do all things through Christ
who strengthens us.
Philippians 4 13

Contents

Foreword

I am so happy that Carey and Pam have been asked to write this particular book. I seriously doubt if there would be many divorces among Christians if they took time to kneel in prayer once each day and each prayed for the other. There can be another time when they pray for children, unsaved friends, ministry and the world situation in general. But I'm speaking of a few minutes when the husband prays exclusively for his wife and she prays exclusively for him. It's impossible to pray this way without looking at things from the other person's point of view.

So whether you pray both ways or just in general for the family and others, it cannot help but bring you closer together.

We do not pray to get things from God, but as we pray God changes us until His will becomes our will.

I know this book will be a blessing to many couples and I hope it will keep many from needlessly calling it quits.

Ruth Bell Graham

Introduction

She writes . . .

One evening shortly before our fifth wedding anniversary, while my husband was occupied with tending the rose bushes in the garden, I went to the front room of our house in Grand Prairie, Texas, just west of Dallas, and took from the bookcase two scrapbooks filled with letters received at the time of my marriage to Carey in September 1986. I settled down in one of our two large navy blue armchairs as the summer sun lowered itself in the huge Texas sky through the window behind me. I do not sit in the front room often. My full-time work as director of the intercessory prayer ministry at Dallas Baptist University means that opportunities to look at scrapbooks full of memories are rare indeed.

But something drew me to the front room now to read the wishes and prayers made by friends and relatives at the time I was about to enter into marriage for the first time at the age of 42. Family and friends all over the world who had supported me through several decades of singleness had sent greeting cards. What joyful messages they contained! Over and over again Carey and I were wished love and joy, peace and happiness, laughter and blessing.

After being engrossed in the scrapbooks for the best part of an hour, I looked through the window at the changing colors of the immense sky and contemplated yet again that satisfying deep joy that, although part of my life for five years now, was somehow forever new. I wondered how many other women had the privilege of being able to say after five years of marriage that as far as they knew not one of the wishes expressed by family and friends had been in vain.

As I had done countless times before, I began to wonder why it was that Carey and I had been given such a harmonious marriage. *Am I speaking too soon?* I thought to myself. After all, five years is a relatively short time. As I gazed at the ever-changing evening skyscape over Grand Prairie, memory took me on an even longer reflective journey.

When I was growing up in Hastings, England, my overriding desire was to have a good marriage and three children, just like my parents, Jim and Gwen Rosewell. As a small child I had heard and understood the Gospel at my home church at St. Leonards-on-sea. The Lord Jesus Christ had died for the sins of the whole world, including mine. Gladly I accepted Jesus as my Savior—but not as Lord. I would not abdicate to Him the throne of my will. What if, I reasoned, God's will should prove different from mine? What if, among other things, it should not be within His will for me to marry? After all, in England at that time there were far more Christian women than there were Christian men. I knew the Bible made it clear that believers should not marry unbelievers. It therefore followed that many Christian women would not marry. If I surrendered my will to God it would mean I would have to be willing never to marry. I did not want to take the risk, for a good marriage was my one aim in life. I had no personal career aspirations whatsoever.

But in 1965, on an ordinary spring evening when I was 21 years old, all that changed. At a retreat of the young people of our church the Lord Jesus Christ claimed me and my will forever. For the first time I saw the price He had paid for me by His death on the cross and I yielded to Him all my will. I prayed: "If You want me to be single in Your service, I will be. I will never seek a marriage partner. If You want me to marry, I will trust You to bring someone to me. I give You all rights to myself."

From that moment of relinquishment, I had a peace I had never known before. I never lost my desire to marry, but as time went by and I remained single, I had the abiding knowledge that I was called to be celibate for a purpose. The Lord's reasons became clearer as the years progressed. From 1968 until 1976 I worked with Brother Andrew, "God's Smuggler" in the Netherlands. The ministry to the "suffering Church," as he called it, behind Iron, Bamboo and Muslim "Curtains," consumed my time and attention—as did learning the Dutch language and culture.

In 1976, I joined Corrie ten Boom as her companion. This meant for me, as it had for her two previous companions, an open-ended, 24-hour-a-day commitment. It was a difficult adjustment for me. I had been used to complete independence in a small apartment of my own in the old Dutch town that housed Brother Andrew's headquarters. Now I was called into a relationship with Tante (Aunt)

Corrie, which I soon learned was one of mutual codependence. We lived, ate and traveled together in a partnership that in many ways, I was sure, must be similar to marriage. My private way of life had ended. Not only was I hardly ever alone (and I had considered aloneness for at least part of the day essential to people with my reflective kind of temperament) but Tante Corrie liked complete openness with her close co-workers. She even opened some of my personal mail, I discovered to my shock. I calmed down when I realized that as her assistant I opened and read *her* private mail. Why should she not do the same with mine?

In August 1978 Corrie, then 86 years old, suffered a stroke, which robbed her of both mobility and speech. During the ensuing five years in her rented house in Placentia, California, I often comforted myself with the thought that, hard though it sometimes was, it was a good thing I was single. How could I have done all the things that Tante Corrie's illness entailed if I had been married? Perhaps, I thought, as I closed the scrapbooks in my lap, the years with Tante Corrie were a kind of training for the life I now led, part of the reason Carey and I have such a harmonious relationship.

The sun had set but Carey was still working in the yard, taking advantage of the relative coolness. I closed the blinds and replaced the scrapbooks on their shelf. Finding myself unwilling to return to the present just yet, I went to another shelf and took down my journals for the years 1983–1986; 1983 had been the year of Tante Corrie's death. I was 39 years old and still had no personal career aspirations. The desire to marry had never left me but there was no panic as I looked toward the future. Although my frequent prayer was that the Lord would give me a good and godly husband, I was prepared for that request not to be granted. Married or single, I wanted to do His will.

After helping care for my mother in England until her death at the end of 1983, I worked with the Southern California Billy Graham Crusade and completed the book *The Five Silent Years of Corrie ten Boom.* Visiting England again at the end of 1985, I went to stay with my sister, Sylvia Baker, and her family at their home in northern England. I had no idea what the future held except that en route back to California I was to keep some speaking appointments in Texas in connection with the publication of my book. At 42 years of age I had no prospect of definite income and no plan beyond the next few weeks.

Having contracted the flu in the bone-chilling English north, I had experienced some depressing days in its aftermath. I was surprised, therefore, to awaken on January 5, 1986, two days before my departure for the United States, with an unusual sense of adventure and anticipation. In the kitchen where my sister was cooking the family's breakfast, she greeted me with the words, "As I prayed for you this morning I had an unusual sense of adventure and anticipation about your future. I wonder what the Lord has in store for you?"

It would not be long before I found out.

Later that month, while in Waco, Texas, I met Carey Moore, an editor for a publishing company, and he soon came to mean more to me than any man I had ever met. After my return to California we continued our friendship by letter, telephone and visits. Two months later we became engaged and looked forward to a September wedding.

During the months of our engagement, I received several pieces of advice from well-meaning women friends.

"Be prepared for a big adjustment," said one. "Marriage at any age requires much change, and it certainly will at forty-two."

Two months before our wedding, I confided to a friend how very much I loved Carey and how I looked forward to joining my life to his. Married for fifteen years, my friend sounded doubtful: "I'd like to hear you speak in the same tones one year from now."

Nothing daunted in my longing to become Carey's wife, and not knowing how to prepare for the threatened difficult adjustment, I decided to enjoy every part of the preparations for middle-aged marriage. At least my years of experience meant that closing bank accounts and finishing other business in preparation for the move to Waco after nine years in California were fairly easily accomplished.

On a bright September day that year of 1986, Carey and I became man and wife. Our honeymoon was the 1500-mile journey between California and Texas, which we took in easy stages, arriving in Waco a week after our wedding day. As I unpacked in the little house that was to become our first home, I thought about the threatened adjustment. It had not yet come. After a month, three months, a year, I was still wondering when it was coming.

Another year went by. I thought of the friend who had been so sure I would be disillusioned by marriage. I wished California were not so far away; I wanted to tell her that far from being disenchanted, I loved and respected Carey more now than when I married him.

I was beginning to see why. He was leading me in the ways of the Lord. Easygoing, he dealt with my much more highly strung nature wisely. He laughed when my flair for drama made a small incident seem of mammoth importance to me. (Tante Corrie had helped me here, too. She used to say, "Child, you must learn to see great things great and small things small.") Carey helped me laugh along with him and so gain perspective. As I noted Carey's treatment of me and saw how he often put my comfort before his own, I found myself coming to understand the Lord Jesus in a new way. One day I came across a verse in the New Testament that spoke to me with a new clarity: "Husbands, love your wives, just as Christ loved the church and gave himself up for her." Carey was showing me the kind of love of which Ephesians 5 tells us.

When Carey came in from the yard, I was keen to tell him about my hour with the scrapbooks. "Do you remember," I asked him as he took a seat in the other navy blue armchair, "how I have always wondered why we never had the difficult adjustment my women friends threatened? I think it's partly because I learned some discipline when I worked for Tante Corrie. And partly because you are kind and forbearing and so often go the second mile on my behalf."

"It's certainly true," Carey responded, "that the difficult disciplines in both our lives helped prepare us to come together. But I think there's a more important reason for the harmony."

"What is it?" I asked, curious.

"The fact that we pray together," replied my husband.

My father, Jim Rosewell, undertook the traditional English father's role at our wedding by giving a speech. A lover of English and the meaning of words, he recalled a conversation from years ago when he was cycling to school in Middlesex, England, with two friends. The teacher had asked the students to define *marriage*, and the three boys were constructing their answers as they pedaled through the countryside.

"One boy," my father recounted, "had heard that 'marriage was the finest of man's estates,' and the other that it was 'the pinnacle of man's delight.' " Nearly sixty years later, at our wedding, Dad said, "Dear Pam and Carey, this is what marriage can be for you if you get it right—the finest of man's estates, an experience beyond compare."

Carey and I believe that marriage is a holy estate in which a man and a woman have an equal share, the closest, deepest, most rewarding of all human relationships. We invite you, therefore, to look with us at what we believe is the way to "get it right." It is our conviction that daily prayer together should be the aim of every Christian couple. We want to share with you why we think so, and what the hindrances are to doing so.

Marriage: "an experience beyond compare"? Is this possible in our day and time? We believe it is!

What Happens
When Husbands
and Wives
Pray Together?

1

Prayer Is Knowing God

> Satisfy us in the morning with your unfailing love,
>   that we may sing for joy and be glad all our days.
> Make us glad for as many days as you have afflicted
>   us, for as many years as we have seen trouble.
> May your deeds be shown to your servants,
>   your splendor to their children.
> May the favor of the Lord our God rest upon us;
>   establish the work of our hands for us—
>   yes, establish the work of our hands.
>
> Psalm 90:14–17

He writes . . .

On a Sunday morning in August 1985 these words from Psalm 90 sprang off the bulletin of Park Street Church, Boston, with special meaning to me.

There were several reasons why the verses seemed to have my name on them that day. I had recently accepted a new job in Texas where I was to start afresh in September. The psalmist's plea for God to "establish" his work was surely mine, too. And I had "seen trouble" in the years just past. Only recently had I stopped grieving over a ship-wrecked marriage; and if I had wanted to choose a word to characterize the previous five years I would have thought *affliction* not an exaggeration. Further, I was keen to see a fulfillment of that cry: "Let Your splendor appear to our children." Although I was separated from my two sons and two daughters, I felt all of the normal feelings of love and of pain and of hope for each of their precious lives. For the Lord to allow His majesty to appear to them summed up my chief prayer for them.

One rather obvious element of Psalm 90, however, seemed to disqualify me from the blessings the psalmist sought. He spoke in the plural: "Make *us* glad . . . years *we* have seen . . . your *servants* . . . *their* children." He asked for the Lord's favor "upon *us*" and that the work "of *our* hands" be established. I was definitely not an "us." After nineteen years of marriage, I had been separated from my wife for four years, divorced for one.

Still, there was a kind of intrigue to those plural expressions. Sitting in the pew that August morning, I prayed silently: *Lord, thank You for these words. I make them my own. Do make me glad according to the days You have afflicted me. Do let Your splendor appear to my children. And do confirm for "us" the work of our hands.* Very real then was my hope that God would bring to me a companion. I believe God allowed me—dare I say inspired me?—to pray with such assurance because He had already given me Pam. In less than half a year I would meet her.

Three months later, in November, launched in my new work as an editor in Waco, Texas, I took a short trip to Marshall in the pine forests of East Texas. Gone was the summer heat, adding to the pleasure of the visit with my cousin Reba who was enjoying retirement in the home where she and her late husband had known much happiness. On Sunday morning I awoke in Reba's guest bedroom and found a heartfelt petition forming itself in my mind. All unplanned and unanticipated, I lay there in that comfortable double bed and decisively asked God for a wife!

January came, time to write out my goals for the new year—I never call them "resolutions." The previous January I had written down eight "prayer concerns" in my journal. Number 7 was: "My longing for someone."

Now, January 3, 1986, I wrote:

> Am reviewing the goals I had for 1985. . . . One un-reached objective is to "find someone" and to reestablish my family. In having Jim [my second son] here, I see this happening. Praise God!

Jim had interrupted his sophomore year in college to come to live with me. On January 4 I headed the journal page: "Goals for 1986." Goal number one was:

> Find the woman who will share my life. I believe God is prompting me (Ecclesiastes 9:9) to believe this, and He has seen my sacrifice and my waiting. I look to Him to bring it about. It is time for Thee to work, O Lord.

The passage of a year had clearly moved this petition to the top of the list! As it turned out, Jim's presence was the key to my meeting Pam. As a newcomer in Waco he was naturally lonely. On Sunday, January 19, Jim and I played tennis—to the satisfaction of neither of us. I found out I could not handle his powerful serves anymore, and I knew he was playing tennis with me because he did not have anyone but his dad to spend time with. I recalled my niece Joan and her church, Highland Baptist, a fellowship of several hundred folk. *There could be a friend there for Jim,* I thought. Why not go that very evening?

That was how Jim and I happened to be sitting in the

third pew at Highland Baptist Church on the evening of January 19 when the pastor announced the visiting speaker: Miss Pamela Rosewell. Pam was beginning a three-week speaking visit in and around Waco. The occasion was the publication of her book *The Five Silent Years of Corrie ten Boom.* In those three weeks, it was I who found a friend as Pam and I got acquainted. (At the restaurant where he was waiting tables Jim did eventually find that good friend we had hoped for.)

On February 8, the day she was due to leave Texas for her home in California, I held Pam's hand and prayed with her. That was our first prayer together that I remember. Our latest one was only hours ago, after breakfast— this being a vacation day as I write. We have tried to maintain the habit of prayer together every day since early in our marriage.

Prayer together, we are convinced, ought to be a priority for every married couple.

It is with plenty of hesitance, however, that we have set out to write a book on this topic. For one thing, lots of Christians—anyone who is not an "us"—might seem excluded. We surely do not want to seem to turn our backs on singles. Pam was single for almost 43 years, and I lived alone for five years before our marriage.

At times, when I was single, I had two close friends as prayer partners. Many Christian singles have that special relationship with at least one person whom they pray with regularly. Women are probably more faithful in this than we men. God's Word, while exhorting us to private prayers, also encourages the child of God to pray with another believer. "Two are better than one" (Ecclesiastes 4:9) applies to praying as well as any other activity that can be shared. Jesus' promises in Matthew—"If two of you shall agree on earth concerning anything . . . **Where two or three are gathered together**"—are made to friends or fellow workers as surely as they are to a husband and wife. In these pages, though, we shall focus on prayer for the married couple—hoping that if you are not married you will find them useful in your life of prayer with another person.

We are diffident about writing such a book as well, because prayer is a very large subject. Praying involves a broad spread of activity and, as we shall see, it has depth to it like that of outer space. But God invites us to know Him, and prayer plays a very large part in that.

We are writing particularly for couples and particularly about prayer as coming to know God. As learners on the pilgrimage of faith, we seek here to offer a witness to how a couple can, by praying, come to know God better. Knowing more of the Father, more of His Son, Jesus Christ, and more of the Holy Spirit—that is our goal in praying.

Pam and I wish we could say that we always have the desire to pray, but we don't. I sometimes open our prayer time by saying, "Lord, I don't really want to pray. There are other things I would rather do. Help me."

We do desire to pray together more now than when we started. The starting place for the seeker is to ask God to make him or her willing to pray. "It is God who works in you to will and to act according to his good purpose" (Philippians 2:13). The writer Henri Nouwen said in *Reaching Out* that "the paradox of prayer is that it asks for serious effort while it can only be received as a gift. We cannot plan, organize or manipulate God, but without careful discipline we cannot receive Him either." We can make a habit of prayer, and develop the discipline, but we can only go so far with that. What we need is what only God can give—the grace of prayer. Until we have allowed God to give this gift, we will find ourselves resorting to prayer last—or, at least, late—rather than responding first to any situation by praying.

In this book, we are seeking to be practical and simple. Many couples who pray together regularly have told us what they have learned. Their stories, we think, will encourage you to pray with more assurance, with greater frequency, with growing effectiveness and with an ever-enlarging knowledge of our loving God.

What comes to mind when we try to define prayer? Asking God for things? Praising Him? Discovering His will for us?

The familiar ACTS formula, meant to help us not neglect any aspect of prayer, is sometimes put forth as a definition:

A — Adoration
C — Confession
T — Thanksgiving
S — Supplication

Such checklists are useful, but what they spell out are activities in prayer, *elements* of praying, not the *essence*. We read recently in the Scripture Union *Daily Notes,* which we use in daily devotions, that "prayer is not an Aladdin's lamp which we rub in order to get what we want. It is the way we seek God's will so that we can align ourselves with it." Such a description of prayer speaks of the activity, for we do have to ask and seek and knock; but it also speaks of the essential nature of prayers—getting ourselves in tune and in line with God and His will.

Our favorite definition of prayer is that it is not about obtaining things from God but about knowing God and coming into His presence.

Job may serve as an example of a man who came to know God. This Old Testament figure lost everything—his cattle, his camels, his servants, his sons and daughters and, finally, his health. But his faith remained firm: "The Lord gave and the Lord has taken away," he could say in the midst of calamity. "Blessed be the name of the Lord."

His faith was strong. But he had not come to know God very well. He had some "friends" who tried to show him why all this had happened to him—but that only proved that they did not know God very well either.

The book of Job is largely a record of Job's prayers and his responses to his "comforters." Sometimes he is on the brink of despair: "I loathe my very life" (10:1); "Why then did you bring me out of the womb? I wish I had died before any eye saw me!" (10:18).

At times he is angry at God: "Know that God has wronged me. . . . Though I cry, 'I've been wronged!' I get no response; though I call for help, there is no justice" (19:6–7).

Job does not know about the enemy of his soul and that Satan has gained permission to put him to the test. The biblical account reveals that God allowed the devil to afflict Job in order to teach the devil that not every man has his price. And Job proves his mettle. No matter how black the circumstances, he refuses to turn his back on his Maker.

But before the book ends we see that God must have had another purpose in allowing Satan to test Job, a purpose as significant as proving to the devil that he could lose. And what was that purpose? Job 42:5–6 gives the answer: "My ears had heard of you but now my eyes have seen you. Therefore I despise myself and repent in dust and ashes."

Now my eyes have seen you. . . . Job did not mean that he had literally laid eyes on God. He meant, rather, that he was perceiving Him with the inner eye. His anguished cries, his disputes with his friends and his thoughtful prayers were leading him to know God. That is what God wants most of all.

Prayer that leads a couple increasingly to the heart of God is prayer worth making time for, even in the most demanding and pressed of schedules. Come with us as we seek to know Him.

2

Why Couples Don't Pray Together

May the Lord answer you when you are in distress;
    may the name of the God of Jacob protect you.
May he send you help from the sanctuary
    and grant you support from Zion. . . .
May he give you the desire of your heart
    and make all your plans succeed.

Psalm 20:1–2, 4

He writes . . .

To explain what Pam and I mean by "couple prayer" it
may help to begin with what we do *not* mean. We do not
mean the "family altar"—a daily time of Bible reading and
prayer as a family—invaluable though that is. We are also
not talking about grace at mealtime, though that is a sound
scriptural practice—and can lead to prayer as a couple.
Nor are we talking about the spontaneous prayers—Pam
calls them "arrow prayers"—we all utter in emergencies.
The cry "Help!" may well lead to daily prayer together,
but such irregular, unplanned, infrequent supplication is
not what we have in mind.

Prayer as a couple may include the children, but that is
not quite what we are speaking of either. Our own daily
time of prayer together may include guests who happen to

be with us. But the type of prayer of which we are speaking does not include anyone else on a regular basis; *it is the
joining of husband and wife regularly—daily if possible—in God's
presence to lift the day's concerns to our heavenly Father and to
remind Him, and ourselves, of those petitions that have been
brought to Him before, for which we continue to wait upon Him.*
The prayer we are speaking of is not a burden of some
kind, a legalistic requirement, a joyless, rigid habit. It is
prayer that satisfies, that brings comfort, the knowledge of
being loved and cared for, of being close to each other and
to God.

Dolly Winthrop, the good-hearted lady who attempted
to talk Silas Marner into churchgoing, described something of what we experience in prayer when she reasoned
with the weaver:

> "Well, Master Marner . . . if you've niver had no
> church, there's no telling the good it'll do you. For I
> feel so set up and comfortable as niver was, when I've
> been and heard the prayers, and the singing to the
> praise and glory o' God . . . and if a bit o' trouble
> comes, I feel as I can put up wi' it, for I've looked for
> help i' the right quarter. . . ."

We would that every couple knew the feeling of being
"set up and comfortable," not only because of prayers
prayed in church, but from their own prayers. That is not
because the prayers of the church are not a great blessing.
But for most people they can be shared only once or twice
a week. New challenges and fears come with every day.
How good it is, therefore, if the couple has "looked for
help in the right quarter" daily, and experienced the
"peace that passes understanding" in their hearts.

But if so much joy and satisfaction is derived from praying together, why don't more couples practice it?

"We never thought of it." Many couples, we find, have never given serious thought to the idea of praying together. They attend church and perhaps prayer meetings, but somehow they have never made a habit of praying together as husband and wife. If you and your spouse are in this number, all that may be needed is for one of you to suggest doing it.

"Nobody does it." A second reason couples do not pray together is that no one they know does it. "Our parents didn't pray together, and we have never known a couple who did," many believers tell us. There seem to be no models for them to follow. An example is a powerful thing, certainly, either positively or negatively. My father and stepmother did not pray together. If they had, I am almost sure that they would have been happier; there would have been a sense of God's presence in our home. And who knows how the lives of us six children would nave been different, what sorrows we might have been spared and what blessings would accrue even to our children because of such prayers? But alas, we did without, as do most homes.

"We don't have time." It didn't take much research to discover another reason why many couples do not pray—lack of time. Prayer gets knocked around and knocked out often in a single individual's life by today's pressures, and even more often in a couple's life, for prayer together requires the meshing of two people's schedules. Kathryn Railey of Redmond, Washington, told us, "I think time is probably the number one reason couples find it difficult to

pray, especially if they have children. You have to con-
sciously make time and look for creative ways to put prayer
into busy schedules."

The world's demands and delights are entirely capable
of squeezing all available time out of each day. And if
there should be a little time left in our hectic hours, the
flesh is by then too weak for anything so demanding as
prayer. Add to this the hatred the devil has toward real
prayer and it is easy to see why husbands and wives so
rarely pray together.

Isn't it peculiar that today when everything from touch-
tone phones to microwave ovens and FAX machines is
geared to save us time, we feel we have so little of it? Henry
Virkler in *Broken Promises,* a book on how Christians become involved in extramarital affairs, says that "our expectations about what we want out of marriage have
increased," but "the time and energy we believe we have
available for our spouses has decreased." Many of us probably believe that time simply does not exist for praying
together.

But is this lack of time a valid reason? We don't think so,
for one reason alone. The busiest people we know make
time for praying together. A surgeon and his wife in Dallas
pray together on waking each morning. A traveling salesman in Missouri told us that even when he is away from
home, he and his wife talk by phone each day—and make
it a point to pray with each other though hundreds of
miles apart. When he is not traveling, they begin each
weekday with prayer—and coffee!—at 5:30 in the morning before their teenage daughter gets up.

Pam and I value time like no other precious commodity,
and we can appreciate certain situations that prevent daily
prayer together. When the early evening—our usual

time—is filled with an engagement or if we have guests over, we do not feel under some law to keep our set prayer time. Our post-dinner prayers on such evenings may be briefer, or missed altogether. In such cases we try to pray together at bedtime. I say "try" because fatigue sometimes rules out a prolonged prayer session. If we are driving to an evening engagement, we share a prayer time in the car. If a trip plays fruit basket turnover with our schedules, we try to be flexible and put prayer with each other high on the day's list of priorities.

The point is that having chosen a time when we will customarily pray together, we do not get bent out of shape if that time is unavailable once in a while, for we do not pray to gain God's favor; our acceptance with God is all grace and is not based on anything we do. If we should notice that other things repeatedly crowd out the chosen prayer time, we will look for another hour, for this loving work of prayer is as necessary to a Christian marriage as talk or food.

As important as flexibility in this matter of time is the *amount* of time involved, especially at first. As with any new habit the number of minutes invested should be small to start with. You probably remember, as I do, throwing yourself into what was to be a new exercise routine by knocking yourself out the first day—and then being so sore for a week that you could not continue even if you had wanted to! Praying together is more important than physical exercise and it is wise not to set ourselves such lofty goals that we get discouraged. As the old adage proclaims, "Inch by inch it's a cinch." As a couple you can surely find *two minutes every day* when you can pray together. Perhaps you will want to embrace or hold hands or kneel. You can start by reading aloud one of the prayers in chapter 8, then mentioning one or two current concerns, keeping the whole undertaking to two minutes. If you would stick to that two-minute regimen for two weeks, you might find not only that you do have time, but that you want to "make" a great deal more for this activity!

But . . . We Can't Pray Together

For some readers, all that we have said so far may seem to be pitifully naïve—or downright dishonest. Pam and I must have just stepped off an alien spaceship or have led very sheltered lives. Certainly we are not acquainted with how marriage is in the real world. . . .

"We're not that intimate with each other." One woman from San Marcos, Texas, says that the most difficult part of couple prayer for her and her husband is being "one in mind and heart." Prayer together may seem impossible because you and your marriage partner lack an intimate relationship. You may each have come to know God, but your marriage lacks the closeness required for the total communication involved in prayer.

We took a poll on whether or not spiritual intimacy is an important part of Christian marriage. The majority of the couples answered yes. One responded, "The most important part." But the wistful answers of some spoke volumes: "No, but I wish it were." "No, but I would like it to be."

It might be argued: Which comes first, prayer together or intimacy? If your relationship is not close as a couple, prayer together will be strained. But if you do not pray together regularly, drawing close will be harder. If each of you desires intimacy, why not pray for it? The wife is often the one who wants a more intimate relationship;

we men are frequently unaware of how emotionally closed we are. The woman in this case can make her private prayers very specific: "Lord, show John my need for spiritual intimacy. Help him recognize and admit his true feelings." At an appropriate moment she may ask her husband to pray with her—not about intimacy, but about some need that he is likely to understand. "Dear, this is bothering me. Would you consider praying with me about this one thing?"

"We can't communicate." Have you ever watched a couple sharing a meal together in a restaurant in complete silence? As one writer put it, "A staleness has crept into their marriage and walls of silence have risen between them." He was describing a secular situation, but many believers experience this stagnant kind of relationship as well. Their motto seems to be: "Come weal or come woe, our status is quo."

If the lines of communication are down in your marriage, prayer can be a means of repairing them. The landscape is strewn with the wreckage of marriages that failed for want of true dialogue. I myself suffered such a failure. Much has been written about techniques of communication, and such helps are valuable. Prayer, however, can be a first, not a last, resort.

First, *pray for your mate*—daily, secretly, earnestly, hopefully and specifically.

Second, *express your love*, cherishing your mate in ways he or she can detect and appreciate.

Third, if you find yourself more ready for couple prayer than your partner, *be patient*, serving the Lord from your heart. Let His joy blow away any tendencies to act the martyr.

Fourth, *seek help* from your pastor, a Christian counselor, from books and articles on communication skills. You may receive this couple praying as a gift in answer to your supplications. But if not, keep true to your vows and watchful in your own private communion with the Lord. "Therefore . . . stand firm. Let nothing move you. Always give yourselves fully to the work of the Lord, because you know that your labor in the Lord is not in vain" (1 Corinthians 15:58).

The experience of Neil and Anne Baker illustrates how communication can break down even between partners accustomed to praying together. Neil, 43, the salesman from Springfield, Missouri, mentioned earlier, recalled what happened to him early in 1991.

"I went through what you'd call a midlife crisis," Neil told us, "starting with pressure at work. Because of the competition, our sales were down; and I, who had been a leader in sales, was being turned down a lot. Rejection of our product contributed to my general feeling of being rejected. At home I kept all this bottled up, believing that Anne, who has been my best friend since before we were married, had withdrawn from me too.

"All this time I was questioning God. I wasn't spending time with Him each day like before and I had stopped praying with Anne. This heaped more rejection and guilt on me. In short, I was not a fun person to be around. It didn't help things that our church seemed mainly interested in money for its building program."

Anne meanwhile grew more and more concerned. She never stopped praying for Neil, but finally one evening she had had all she could take. Their daughter had gone upstairs to bed, leaving them alone in the living room. Anne made her move: "Honey," she said, "I love you, but

I don't know how to talk to you anymore. What's bothering you?"

"I wasn't feeling much sympathy for Neil," she admitted to us. "I thought everything was great for him. He had a good job with the company he had worked for for twenty years. He had a wife and daughter who loved him, a beautiful home and, most important, a relationship with God. I couldn't see why he was so unhappy.

"When we talked that evening, Neil asked me to read a chapter in *Men in Mid-Life Crisis* by Jim Conway, which hit several chords on how he was feeling. Then he began to open up and talk about how things were at work, and of his own doubts about the Lord. When he saw what damage he had done to our relationship by keeping everything inside, he began to talk. It was wonderful."

Neil recalls: "Once Anne drew me out and really began to listen to me, I found I could share my feelings with her. We were close again, before that evening ended. From there it was an easier step for us to find time again for real prayer together. It was right for Anne to ask what was wrong and to take the lead in getting us back to praying, because work consumes a man. Had we kept praying together during those six months when I was having a difficult time, Anne would have understood what I was going through."

Neil and Anne found that when they were not talking about things together, a barrier arose that prevented real prayer. Neil's fears and self-doubts were not "safe" subjects to share with his wife—and communication suffered. Which of course brings up another reason why couples don't pray together.

"We're not open with each other." Prayer with another person requires that we be self-disclosing and vulnerable.

'To pray together means being willing to be transparent," our pastor commented one day. "A man or woman won't open up and truly express what's on the heart unless both marriage partners accept one another just as they are, failings and all." Friends of ours who have been married 28 years point out that this sort of openness "takes time."

Only in recent years have I myself become more open in prayer. Tracking my own history, I trace the change to finding friends whom I trusted.

Neil was one of those friends. He himself had gone through a divorce, which helped him understand my pain and confusion when my own family broke up. At his initiative, Neil and I would meet occasionally for supper at a restaurant on the Garden State Parkway in New Jersey—which meant a half-hour drive for him in the rush hour—and then we would go outside to some quiet spot and pray. We prayed for my needs and his, for my children and other people, and I found myself free to be myself in his presence.

At the same time I found a group who prayed at lunchtime at work, and I became a part of a weekly home group of people from my church. Being single and a newcomer in each of these groups, I made the decision early on to tell my new friends about the sad breakup of my marriage. My willingness to share where I had failed broke the ice and allowed me to tell them from time to time about other needs and to receive their counsel and encouragement. These people were not afraid to shed tears and share real burdens. In that accepting circle of friends I experienced liberty to be vulnerable in prayer.

"He's too proud to pray."/"She's got this superior attitude." Women, as I mentioned, are often more ready for spiritual intimacy than men. Husbands can find this prospect threatening. A man who thinks he must always appear strong and in control will shy away from prayer with others, even with his wife. This is unfortunate, for at times even the strongest are not strong enough. A man may not be able to let certain people see him weak or dependent, but with Christ's help he can certainly learn to be himself with his wife, and his wife to be herself with him.

We are stronger, Pam and I, for sharing in prayer together. But neither of us would want to continue if either one assumed a superior or judgmental attitude. Prayer together requires donning the cloak of humility, which may be another reason—and a basic one—why husbands and wives resist it. Someone has said, "The ground is level at the cross." If we want to succeed in this kind of prayer, we must come to it with the knowledge that we are no better and no worse than our partners.

"The children interrupt us." When we sent out the set of questions on prayer to nearly one hundred couples we wondered how those with children—especially small children—would answer. Obviously if they had been praying together before they began their families, adjustments had to be made. Some admitted that with the arrival of children their prayer time together sort of evaporated, while others incorporated the youngsters into the practice.

Kell and Ann McCaskill of Arlington, Texas, wrote that, for them and their three sons, "breakfast has always been a special time—a *together* time that became a priority for all of us, regardless of increasingly busy schedules. It seems natural that this, too, became our favorite prayer time, as a family and now as a couple. Our most precious prayer pattern became the habit of each of the five of us praying aloud at the breakfast table for another one about whatever was upcoming for him that day. Now that Kell and I are in the empty nest stage (having three daughters-in-law and four grandchildren) we continue the tradition by each of us praying daily for one of the other eleven."

The McCaskills raised their children in a time when families could live more easily on one income than many can today. We wondered what happened to prayer time in the home where both parents work full-time. A couple we know in Flower Mound, near Dallas, Chuck and Pat Bianco, have handled the situation this way: "After our Marriage Encounter weekend, Chuck and I began to dialogue daily (the Marriage Encounter technique of first writing out, then discussing, feelings). We had our prayer time in conjunction with the dialogue finding that our dialogue enhanced our prayers, and vice-versa. The three children knew from the time they were small that Mommie and Daddy dialogued each day and needed some time for themselves alone. They would answer the phone if it rang and learned that this was a time not to interrupt, except in an emergency."

Chuck and Pat work in offices near each other and so can commute together on most days. "This gives us additional prayer time in the car on our way to and from work."

Other friends—Eng and Lina Go—have a small daughter, Caressa, two years old. Indonesians, they are part of a fellowship of Indonesian Christians in America. Pam and I wondered what the addition of a baby would do to their private prayer life. Eng responded: "It is almost impossible to demand cooperation from Caressa. She is beginning to understand the posture of praying, but not what it means. And she can stay in that posture about fifteen seconds! What we do is divide the prayer topics and then take turns praying. Whoever is not praying is watching Caressa As for Caressa, she will play with her toys as long as one of us is on call. By now we are getting used to praying like this and it doesn't disturb our concentration."

I suppose Eng and Lina are not the first parents who have learned a second meaning of the admonition "watch and pray."

"We're not at the same place spiritually." It is a rare marriage, in fact, where the partners' spiritual growth proceeds in lockstep. One may have known the Lord longer or developed his or her prayer life to a greater degree. Margie Bondurant, a schoolteacher in Minneapolis, describes a plight that is perhaps typical. Margie recalls that when the children were young she and her husband, Gregg, tried devotions, consisting of a story from the Bible and prayer by each in turn. "But it was not a good plan," she confesses. "I forced it and it lacked the naturalness I believe a shared decision would have had." Today she says "it has been necessary for me to step back and be quiet—but prayer together is coming!"

If both husband and wife are seeking God and His will for their marriage, it matters little if one is "ahead" of the other. Being a Christian is not about being number one; it is about preferring another before myself. If the man is more mature spiritually, praying with his wife is for him an excellent exercise in patience and meekness. The same is true for the woman who is more apt at prayer. When I stumble for the right word in prayer, Pam never betrays impatience. She waits silently, praying in her heart. We have learned to take our faulty language and incomplete understanding to God in prayer together, thankful for the assurance of Romans 8:26: "The Spirit helps us in our weakness. We do not know what we ought to pray for, but the Spirit himself intercedes for us with groans that words cannot express."

Even though one marriage partner may be more experienced in these matters, on any given day a dozen things can happen to cause one to be bold in prayer, the other timid. The "more spiritual" one may have fallen prey to some temptation, or the weaker one may have seen the Lord work in a special way, so both prayer partners can bless each other and neither one bear the responsibility of always being the "leader."

"It would become a ritual." This is a frequent objection and an important one. But being aware of the danger, I think, is half of the solution. True, God is against mere ritual in prayer. But ask yourself, Is conversation at mealtime a ritual? We do it daily. Is it not true that each day brings its own variation on familiar themes?

In chapter 7, we describe the different focus Pam and I have for intercession on each of the six days of the week, to keep our prayer time from becoming routine. Also, we don't depend on written prayers. Instead we use plain speech in much the same way we talk with each other. There are other ways we seek variety. Sometimes we pray upstairs in our bedroom, other times while sitting on the living room sofa; sometimes we read from a devotional book or sing a hymn. Being flexible and creative can prevent our daily prayers from falling into tedium and rote.

"I could never pray aloud in someone else's presence!" Shyness in prayer is a real obstacle—but not an unconquerable one. The fear of a stumbling and hesitant delivery may be especially intense when one's partner can pray

eloquently and naturally. A husband told us, "Words don't
come as easily for me as they do for my wife." I do not
recall having this problem, for I grew up in a church that
encouraged its young people to lead in prayer. If anything, I have had to learn not to pray to the gallery, but to
God alone. For those of us accustomed to praying in public, a few moments of silence are often necessary in order
to direct one's prayer to God and not to anyone who happens to be present.

An inexperienced or shy pray-er can learn to pray aloud
with another person if that person is a friend. And what
better companion in prayer than one's own spouse? The
more experienced partner, in this situation, should honor
the learner's need for time to voice a prayer, even a whispered one, and should temper his or her own flow of
words so as not to intimidate an easily daunted mate. This
art of praying with others can be mastered in time, though
shyness may always be with us. Kara Bradley, a young
mother in Marietta, Georgia, confesses that she is still
sometimes shy while praying with her husband, Jim: "I see
prayer as so personal that I sometimes feel embarrassed at
my self-disclosure." Let Jesus' promise encourage us to
break through the shyness barrier: "If two of you agree on
earth about anything that they may ask, it shall be done for
them by My Father who is in heaven" (Matthew 18:19,
NASB).

Pat Bianco, who learned with her husband, Chuck, how
to maintain a daily prayer time while raising three active
children, had to overcome her shyness when first praying
with Chuck. "Praying together out loud seemed awkward
at first," she recalls. "We both felt self-conscious. It was
something we both wanted, however, and we stuck with it.
I enjoyed listening to Chuck pray and felt closer to him as

a result. I began to cherish those moments listening to him come before the Father as a child and lay himself bare before Him, and I felt privileged to be a part of those intimate moments."

Chuck at the outset felt obliged to sound fluent. "But when I was able to put my pride aside, the Lord and my Pat helped me to open up and eliminate the defense mech anisms."

"Listening to Chuck pray," Pat says, "also helped me to know how to pray for him during the day, what his needs were, and to be more aware of lifting him up in prayer when we were apart. We began couple prayer by praying together at night We still pray together before bedtime each evening and also pray as we drive into work together. For us, it is the best way to begin and end each day."

In this chapter we have talked about some of the more common reasons why Christian couples don't pray together regularly. We have considered the absence of models, the lack of time, the breakdown of communication and intimacy, the inequality of spiritual development, the risk of ritual, the barrier of shyness. Perhaps you have reasons that we have not even touched upon. Kathy Bruner of Spokane, Washington, told us: "I find *praying* difficult, not the *together* part!" That honest statement may go a long way in explaining why many couples do not pray. She added: "Yes, it is hard to make the time. And yes, it does become routine so quickly. I tend to get bogged down in details, informing the Lord of stuff He knows so well! But basically, even after many years, I just find praying hard." The difficulties, however, don't keep Kathy and her husband, Dale, from doing it!

Prayer together is not a "side issue" in a Christian marriage. It requires a commitment as surely as going to work demands consistent commitment. And it requires that each partner be a Micah 6:8 kind of Christian—seeking to do the right thing, showing compassion and walking humbly with God. In the next chapter we will look at another requirement: What is so special about *daily* prayer? Wouldn't weekly or occasional prayer together achieve the same ends?

3

Why Pray Together Daily?

Day by day,
Dear Lord, of Thee three things I pray:
  to see Thee more clearly,
  love Thee more dearly,
  follow Thee more nearly,
Day by day.
       St. Richard of Chichester (13th century)

He writes . . .

We must be honest. We did not immediately, on being married, begin daily prayer together. And though it is now enough of a habit that we can speak of it as such, we have only been "at it" for some four years.

Every evening, with the frequent exception of Sundays, we intend to pray together after the evening meal. Unless an engagement interferes, we are usually able to keep this "appointment with God." We have a regular place—the front room, where Pam and I can sit comfortably in armchairs. But often as not, we may sit on the sofa or remain in the comfy, blue-cushioned chairs at the little oak dining table. From this, you can tell that we don't lie on nails for prayer time. Prayer is work, so it seems best to choose a setting where the labor is not made harder by physical discomfort.

We don't turn straight to the clean-up after supper, and we don't get on the phone at that time. Our "equipment" consists only of our prayer notebook—a white, three-ring binder—and a pen. Pam will occasionally bring Spurgeon's *Evening by Evening* to our prayer time, or we will sing from the hymnbook. But usually we sit down side by side and open the notebook to the pages for that day of the week. (See chapter 7.) The pages contain photos, letters and brief entries—a name, a specific request and perhaps a date. We look over our list, then pray, usually for twenty to thirty minutes.

How did we come to pray together daily?

In part because we had already formed the habit of daily prayer as individuals. When we married, each of us had been following for many years the daily discipline of Bible reading and prayer upon rising. Individually, we had stumbled often in our first attempts. Pam has told me how difficult it was for her. Her main problem was with rising. I was very inconsistent, too, when I first tried to develop a personal devotional life; I just could not discipline myself to get up in time to devote some undistracted time to God. But the Lord, speaking through my conscience and through the lives of more mature believers, kept bidding me, and gradually I began to be a regular in the ranks of those seeking Him early.

We still believe that this individual morning quiet time is essential to the Christian life. When we seek God before anything else, putting the day in His omnipotent hands, we tune our ears to hear Him throughout the day, and find ourselves actually being renewed bit by bit, day by day, into that "new man" and "new woman" He intends for us to become.

Adding to this a time of daily couple prayer had a personal impetus for Pam and me. Because we found each other rather late, Pam in her forties and I in my fifties, we have a super-charged desire to share all of our lives with each other. Life is too short to miss doing together whatever we can, including communion with God.

Yet it matters little why we—just one happy couple— have developed a prayer life together if there remain no compelling reasons for every Christian couple to do so. We suggest that several compelling reasons can be offered, which may be called *convictions for daily prayer as couples.* The order in which they are listed here is not important, but we think these, at least, are the mandates for daily prayer together:

1. The crying, crushing needs around us.
2. The weakened, threatened state of Christian marriage.
3. The desire to be obedient.
4. The promised blessing of God's presence when two pray together.
5. The joy and added grace that come in seeing God answer prayer.
6. The help prayer gives in resolving conflict.
7. The door prayer opens into intimacy.
8. The fellowship with God prayer creates.

1. The Needs Around Us

When we first set out to consider the why of daily prayer for couples, we listed God's promised presence and blessing as reason number one. That well may be the primary reason. But we confess that we were not so compelled by the love of God, and the desire to worship Him, that we carved out a prayer time in our daily schedules. Rather, we began praying together because of the needs in our own lives and in the lives of others, and in the wider world. Our early prayer times together were generously seasoned with heartfelt thanksgivings to God for His mercy and kindness, but the thing that most often motivated us to prayer was the encountering of problems.

Pam and I had financial needs, for example. Before we were married, Pam had lived on a modest income in southern California. In 1983, after the death of Corrie ten Boom and the closing of their "Shalom House," Pam purchased the 1977 Chevrolet that Corrie's ministry had obtained for Corrie's use. "Home" for her was a room with a Christian family. Meanwhile, in New Jersey, where I worked as a book editor, my situation was similar to hers. I also had only enough income to afford a room in someone else's home. My possessions consisted of the 1979 Chevrolet I had bought from my stepmother, some books, a coffee table and a wrought-iron dinette table with four chairs. I was making child support payments for my son Jim, sixteen, and my two daughters, Stephanie, thirteen, and Kathryn, nine, and meeting medical and dental expenses.

The new job in Waco, Texas, afforded me the opportunity of leasing an apartment. To have my own bedroom furniture and sofa and easy chair—each piece well broken-in—was wonderful fun for me. It was in this upstairs apartment that I entertained Pam in 1986 when she came back to Waco to visit after we were engaged. We still smile at the simple meal of meatloaf, served on the wrought-iron table. Through combining our small savings we were able to make a down payment on a modest brick home on Meadow Road and move in after the wedding. Pam was delighted to have a home of her own, and she made it cozy with what we owned and had been given.

Jim, who had been sharing an apartment with a friend, moved in with us in the spring of 1987, and his move made the three of us feel like family. That autumn, Pam began writing *Safer Than a Known Way* and Jim searched around for the college where he would continue his education. Meanwhile, his older brother, Jon, went from duty with the U.S. Navy to the University of Washington. Though he had received a scholarship from the Navy, we knew that Jon would need help from time to time.

In February 1988 I wrote in my journal: "We are so blessed, but we are always just almost out of money."

Money woes came up constantly in our prayers together back then. The spring of 1988 saw us pass two milestones in our life together. Pam completed her book, and the company I worked for announced we would be moving to Dallas in September. A welcome surprise came in the summer, which helped us see how we could afford to live in the Dallas–Fort Worth area. Pam was invited to join the staff of Dallas Baptist University, meaning that we would have two incomes.

In Dallas we had the first real conflict in our marriage, and it was exacerbated by the differences between our two ways of looking at things. It was September, and Pam, Jim and I had moved into an apartment not far from Dallas Baptist University. On the weekend before I was to resume work for my company in its new location, a cable television technician arrived at our apartment to hook up a service that Jim had ordered. Pam took a dislike, as I interpreted it, to the technician and was not going to let him proceed. She felt that Jim was being exploited, for the man was installing a more sophisticated cable system than Jim, who had mainly wanted a sports channel, had agreed to. For my part, though I did resent his disrespectful attitude toward Pam, I thought the man was only doing his job. I let him make the connection.

That night and all the next morning, Pam and I were uncharacteristically silent. But on the way back to our apartment after church, we talked. She was depressed and in tears. She helped me see my not taking her side in the matter of the TV man was only part of the problem. She was concerned about our finances. She was worried about not having enough money to make a trip we planned later in the month, and she was even more worried that I did not seem to worry about it at all. We told each other our failings. I had been insensitive to her strong intuitions the night before, and had not protected her from fears, unfounded though I might have considered them. We made up, and in my journal went that day a record of a telling decision: "O Lord, we stand against Satan and take authority in Jesus to keep free to love each other and to serve You with a whole heart. We are now taking more time to read the Word and pray and wait on God."

Financial needs continued, especially as we faced the decision about buying a house in the expensive Dallas area, but those cares were as nothing compared to our longings for my daughters, Stephanie and Kathy. In February 1988 I had written: "Lord, sometimes I feel a burden for the children that I cannot bear."

Early in the period of separation from my first wife, a wall had begun forming between my daughters and me. By the time of the divorce in 1984, I could feel a painful distance between me and each of them.

That summer I had planned to take both daughters with me to Texas for a family wedding. It was a crushing blow to me when my girls did not consent to my wishes—in part because it was so unlike my own experience as a child.

Daddy ran things in our home, at least after Mother's early death. I would never have thought of not agreeing to something he desired. Although my father was no model of the sensitive parent, I was reared to obey him, and it hurt that I no longer had very much influence over my daughters. I was aware, of course, that they too were hurting. In prayer I called to mind John 3:27: "A man can receive only what is given him from heaven." I decided that I must respect my daughters' feelings, and that I could trust God to "give" them to me for the trip, or to withhold them, as He judged best. In the end one of the girls agreed to go and we had a satisfying father-daughter time.

At about this time it became my practice to fast and pray at noon once a week, particularly asking God for my previously close ties with both girls to be restored. The idea came to me after hearing author and psychologist James Dobson describe how he fasted once a week in order to pray for his own children. Every Tuesday for two years I took my lunch hour to go walking in the neighborhood near my office, offering up prayers for my daughters and my sons.

For Jon, as for the girls, my petition was for reconciliation. My prayers for Jim were along different lines, for we had remained close as he reached adulthood.

When Jim moved with us to Dallas, he was still covering up the hurt he felt in seeing his family break apart, and it took a while before he would allow anyone to penetrate his "cool" exterior. Pam loved all of the children from the start. But because Jim lived with us, he experienced that love daily. And God used Pam's unconditional acceptance, and the young Christian friends Jim was meeting at Dallas Baptist University, where he matriculated in the fall of

1989, to bring him to thoroughly solid ground in his walk with God.

I have written about these personal matters to illustrate the kinds of need that led Pam and me to daily prayer together. As a friend put it, "My husband and I come together consistently in prayer only when something major is going on."

Our friends Chuck and Pat Bianco faced one of these major crises in 1991. As we were beginning this book their teenage son, Chuck, Jr., developed abnormal swelling in his lower legs. For several weeks we prayed with them for the physician to be able to discover what was wrong. Pat wrote of their ordeal after their son had undergone open-heart surgery:

> Though there were difficult and trying times, we were so conscious of the Lord's presence with us and His loving arms around us. Even when I slept at the hospital for four weeks in Chuck, Jr.'s, room, Chuck and I never missed praying together each day and coming aside together to be with the Lord. On the morning of his open-heart surgery the words *Be still and know that I am God* leapt out of Scripture at us and we felt a peace that He was in control.
>
> When we look back now at all the hurdles we overcame we ask ourselves, "How did we do it?" But then we realize we did not do it at all. His grace was there to draw on each time we needed it. We held on tightly to each other and to Him and we got our miracle, a healthy son again. He carried us when we needed to be carried, He loved us tenderly through His people, and through all the turmoil He guided us to the right doctors and the right hospital. We can trace His footprints through all that transpired those seven months.

The burdens that others around us were bearing would often make our problems seem very small. Family members and friends, and those of whom we knew only by way of television and newspaper reports, became the subjects of our prayer together. Like other believers, we found ourselves meeting need on every hand, called by necessity to maintain prayer lists and persevere in daily intercession.

2. The Threatened State of Christian Marriage

She writes . . .

Another compelling reason why Carey and I seek to pray together every day is our conviction that marriage itself is under assault as never before.

When on September 13, 1986, we became man and wife in Rose Drive Friends Church in Yorba Linda, California, we exchanged the most binding of vows. I have an abnormally soft voice, but I tried my hardest to project it that afternoon hoping the very volume would underline the intent of my heart when I said:

"I, Pam, take you, Carey, to my wedded husband, to have and to hold from this time forward; for better for worse, for richer for poorer, in sickness and in health, according to God's holy ordinance. . . ."

With all my heart I want to keep that vow before God, before Carey and before the Church. I believe God has been very gracious to us and blessed us with a strong marriage, but I want to remember the warning in the Bible, "Let the person who thinks he stands take heed lest he fall" (see 1 Corinthians 10:12).

In its special edition on the American family in 1990,

Newsweek magazine reported: "The divorce rate has doubled since 1965, and demographers project that half of all first marriages made today will end in divorce. Six out of ten second marriages will probably collapse."

Lest we comfort ourselves with the thought that these are merely secular statistics, let's remember that things considered unthinkable by Christians several decades ago are now thought normal, including the terrible sin of divorce. In his book *The Frog in the Kettle*, George Barna predicts: "By 2000, Americans will generally believe that a life spent with the same partner is both unusual and unnecessary. We will continue our current moral transition by accepting sexual relationships with one person at a time—'serial monogamy'—to be the civilized and moral way to behave."

God's ideal, one man with one woman for life, is the ideal Christians are called to uphold and protect. But it is becoming more acceptable to change partners as the Church, instead of upholding the truth of the Word of God, is adapting to the climate of the age, allowing the world to squeeze us into its mold. Since no Christian is exempt from the danger, Carey and I and every Christian couple must be on the alert every day of our lives together.

My husband and I believe that daily prayer as a couple helps make our marriage stronger and helps keep us from sinning against God and each other. Ken and Brenda Barker, friends in Lewisville, Texas, parents of three adopted girls, declare: "We have never seen a couple we knew, one who prayed together regularly, encounter serious marital difficulties. It's that simple . . . and yet that profound."

We do not make it a daily prayer that God will protect our marriage from the prevailing danger, but we do make it a frequent one. We bring our vows to mind in a number of ways. Sometimes we repeat our formal marriage commitment to each other to remind us of our binding promise. At other times I look at Carey's wedding ring and rehearse privately the promise I made when I placed it on his finger. I often examine my own wedding ring and bring to mind the exact words of the promise Carey made to me. It is a personal desire of mine never to remove my wedding ring for any reason. Carey placed it there in the presence of God. When attending the weddings of friends it is our habit to hold hands as we sit with the other guests. As the woman takes her vows I squeeze Carey's hand tighter. When the man takes his, Carey indicates by the pressure of his hand that he too is renewing his promise to me.

We two disciples remember another disciple who failed the Lord when he was sure he would not. "I'll never deny You, Lord!" Peter promised. But Peter broke his promise, and we remind ourselves of the warning Jesus gave him, "Watch, and pray, so that you will not enter into temptation."

3. The Desire to Be Obedient

He writes . . .

Nowhere that Pam and I know of does God command husbands and wives to pray together. Matthew 18:19–20 comes close to being such a command, though Jesus does not limit the "two" who agree in prayer to husbands and wives. Those verses are at least strong encouragement for married couples to believe God will answer their prayers.

Adam and Eve, our first parents, walked and talked with

God in the Garden of Eden. Their conversations with their Maker before the fall present a pattern for all subsequent couples to follow. In 1 Samuel 1:19, while Hannah and Elkanah, parents of Samuel, are in Shiloh, we read, "Then they arose early in the morning and worshiped before the Lord, and returned again to their house in Ramah."

It would be lovely if the book of Acts or the epistles gave examples of Christian couples praying together. But only veiled references exist. One is in Paul's first letter to the Corinthians in the context of a discussion of the sexual side of marriage:

> The wife's body does not belong to her alone but also to her husband. In the same way, the husband's body does not belong to him alone but also to his wife. Do not deprive each other except by mutual consent and for a time, so that you may devote yourselves to prayer.   1 Corinthians 7:4–5

Whether this is to be individual prayer or couple prayer, however, Paul does not specify. Peter too touches on prayer in giving advice to husbands:

> Husbands, in the same way be considerate as you live with your wives, and treat them with respect as the weaker partner and as heirs with you of the gracious gift of life, so that nothing will hinder your prayers.
>   1 Peter 3:7

Again, is this prayer *with* the partner, or does Peter make such a distinction?

Eng and Lina Go came recently to the conviction that to pray together is a mark of their obedience. Eng says:

Yes, it's true there is no specific command for a couple to pray together. If we look more closely, however, into the context of prayer in the Scriptures, and even more into the whole context of the Word of God, we have to conclude that God commands a Christian couple to pray together. The command "pray for one another" in the New Testament was given to and in the context of a community of believers. What is the nucleus of that community of believers? Obviously, family units. And what is the nucleus of a family? Parents—the husband and wife. It is more obvious when we understand how dear a family is to God, it being the first institution He created.

Joel and Maria Shuler of Stone Mountain, Georgia, state succinctly this matter of obedience: "God brought us together and so it is important for us to approach Him together in prayer. The only way we can develop couple spirituality is to pray together."

4. The Blessing of God's Presence

"The Lord gives strength to his people; the Lord blesses his people with peace" (Psalm 29:11). This verse holds special promise for couples, for wives and husbands often find themselves needing strength and peace. The promise comes from the Father, and I believe it is realized as we come to Him in prayer.

Centuries after the psalmist wrote those words, Jesus declared the special blessing of God upon corporate prayer:

Again I tell you this: if two of you agree on earth about any request you have to make, that request will

> be granted by my heavenly Father. For where two or
> three have met together in my name, I am there
> among them.　　　　　　Matthew 18:19–20, NEB

What immense promises these are! Not only will God give what is requested, He will give of Himself, His very presence, to those who pray together.

Let's consider each of these two blessings in turn.

First, that God grants requests cannot be doubted. Every day a million testimonies could be added to the myriad already piled up through all of history—testimonies to the effect that *God answers prayer.* Just today, Larry, a student at Dallas Baptist University, called across the campus lawn to me, "I prayed for rain, and we sure got it!" Yes, we surely have—an unseasonable and totally surprising three days of rain in north Texas in mid-August.

Corrie ten Boom told her audiences: "Be careful what you pray, because the Lord hears, and the Lord answers."

Couples who pray together know this is true. But for everyone who reports prayers answered, someone can report that no answer has come. Does that mean that Jesus did not speak the truth, that God cannot be trusted? No. For as we pray with another, we are doing more than engaging in a conversation with God. We are doing battle and there are forces against our prayers. We don't have to overcome God's unwillingness, for it is He who is inspiring our prayers. But if we pray for something long enough, chances are we will find our prayers changing. Sometimes this is because God, over time, is sifting our motives. We may have been wrong about what we were asking, because we had not seen what God was about. Other times Satan has thrown such chains and defenses around the object for which we pray that years of intercession and hosts of prayer warriors are required to call down the fire of God and cut through the obstacles.

Above all, as we said at the outset, prayer is at its deepest *knowing God*. God is known through the crucible of a life given (and not giving up!) to prayer. It appears that God would rather that we come to know Him than that we have our prayers answered right away. Would we seek Him on Wednesday if we got what we wanted on Tuesday?

The second part of this promised blessing to two who pray is that God will make His presence known. Again and again my journal records moments like this one from August 29, 1987: "Pam and I read Psalm 139 with coffee on the back porch, and in prayer we really felt God's presence. I think that prayer time gave us super energy for the whole day."

Now, I may have truly sensed God's presence, or I may have merely enjoyed the morning coffee with Pam, who I think is rather divine, and mistaken those happy feelings for God's being near.

The *feeling* of God's nearness is somewhat akin to the inspiration artists and writers experience. I once heard a writer say that while the craft of writing is ninety percent perspiration and ten percent inspiration, she banked on the inspiration. She made it her business to be at her typewriter every day, explaining that she wanted to be there when the inspiration came!

The couple that prays regularly together will, according to God's promise, always have the blessing of His presence. That is not to say they will always sense it, however. They are like the writer—ninety percent perspiration, ten percent inspiration. But at times, they will know that God is very near, a palpable Presence they were not aware of only a short while before. This communing with God, whether felt or unrealized, is as marvelous a reason for prayer together as is the delight in seeing prayers answered.

5. The Joy and Added Grace that Come in Seeing God Answer Prayer

Probably the best-known professor among the faculty of Dallas Baptist University is Dr. Fred A. White. An institution in himself, this white-haired gentleman has taught at D.B.U. for 26 years. An inveterate runner at age 79, Dr. White is a frequent winner in the sprints among his age group. He has his sights set on running in the senior Olympics and the world veterans track and field championships in 1993. But Dr. White is best known on campus for his ready smile. He exemplifies the warmth and friendliness for which Texas is famous.

He said to Pam recently, "I don't understand prayer, but I believe in it and I practice it, and it works."

There are indeed mysterious aspects to prayer; we will probably never understand how our prayers—feeble or fervent—can make a difference in the scheme of things. But in one sense, there is only one mystery concerning prayer.

It is no mystery that the students at D.B.U. gather at the cafeteria three times a day; or that drivers pull into the local gas station and put an odd-shaped nozzle into a hole in the side of the car, only to return a few days later to repeat the process.

No, the mystery would be if people did *not* show up when meals were ready, or if drivers failed to fill their tanks when gas was available.

The mystery about prayer is that more of us do not resort to it every day for the nourishment and power it provides.

The main effect upon us, when we see God's hand move and know that our prayers have played a part, is joy. Wonderful joy. Abounding joy. Didn't Jesus promise as much? "Ask and you will receive, and your joy will be complete" (John 16:24).

Martin Luther said, "Prayer is a powerful thing, for God has bound and tied himself thereto. None can believe how powerful prayer is, and what it is able to effect, but those who have learned it by experience." Betty and Gene Addison of Ridgewood, New Jersey, who have maintained their daily prayer life together for 22 years, know by experience not only that prayer is powerful but that "there is more power in prayer together than separately."

We have labeled this fifth reason for daily prayer "the joy and *added grace* that come through answered prayer." By this we mean that faith is renewed through a present experience so we can trust God in future storms.

Someone has said, "Prayer *works*. Prayer *is* work. Prayer works on *you*."

We don't usually like to speak of prayer in this way, that it "works," as though prayer were a mechanical thing. But the expression does convey a truth, and so we will bear with it for the time being. It will be clear to all who set themselves to the habit of prayer that prayer is work. But we believe "work" is not a dirty word, a thing to be avoided. In this book we hope so to present the value and significance of prayer to couples that all will be willing for the work. But consider the last part of the axiom—prayer works on you.

Have you prayed for something and seen God answer

your prayers? Most of us who have known the Lord for any time can say yes. And what did that experience do for you? Did it not encourage you to trust God even more? The Word says, "He gives us more grace" (James 4:6).

I have been given a healthy body and known little in the way of serious illness. But in 1990 a small growth on one vocal cord made surgery necessary twice—once in April, and again in August when the granuloma reappeared. When Pam and I faced the first surgery, we were concerned that the tissue might prove malignant. Thankfully, it was not. Each time we and our praying friends sought God for His healing, apart from surgery or by means of surgery. We concluded that, since the growth persisted, we should submit to the surgery, believing that God had provided it as a means for my healing.

After the second operation I continued to see the doctor from time to time. Seven months later, in March 1991, he found a growth reappearing. I was not surprised, for I could feel something like a tiny pea in my vocal cord area. This time, the doctor asked me to return to him in thirty days, adding: "Let's pray that the Lord will reduce it in size or make it go away altogether."

Pam and I followed his suggestion and for the next thirty days, each evening at bedtime, Pam laid a hand on my throat and prayed for my healing. In April when I returned to the doctor, to the relief of all of us he found the growth reduced in size.

Five months later the pesky problem now seems to be making a comeback, for I can feel "something" there. We don't know yet what this will lead to, but the experience of daily, specific prayer last spring has brought us to the point where we can lay hold of God's power with more confidence. He has added grace. And we find that this grace that has been granted through our personal difficulty—albeit a small one—is effective in adding bold faith to our prayers for others.

The psalmist says, "Taste and see that the Lord is good." This "tasting" of the Lord's abundant goodness by seeing Him intervene in the lives of His children does wonders for one's motivation. It makes us want to return again and again to Him, the "Fount of every blessing," and lift our voices in daily prayer together.

6. The Help Prayer Gives in Resolving Conflict

Every marriage has the potential for conflict. As somebody whimsically put it, "Where two or three selfish people are gathered together—a fight is always possible!"

In *Love for a Lifetime* James Dobson says, "It is impossible for me to overstate the need for prayer in the fabric of family life." He adds, "Being able to bow in prayer as the day begins or ends gives expression to the frustrations and concerns that might not otherwise be ventilated."

We have found in five years of marriage—Pam smiles and says, "Now we can give advice"—that conflicts arise, but that they need never cause a fight. True, we have been given an exceptionally harmonious relationship. We share a lot in common and our similar interests and tastes aid in maintaining that harmony.

Both of us, for instance, are "morning people," and thus tend to begin the day on the same schedule. Our "connectedness" continues while we are apart; often Pam will phone me at the exact moment I'm phoning her! We both enjoy hot tea—with milk, no sugar—before breakfast, and I have learned that if the world is about to get the better of us, we can meet almost any challenge if first we make a pot of tea. (Thank God for the British!) Each of us enjoys traveling and hiking, reading and keeping a daily journal, singing and silence, chocolate, Chinese food and watching Wimbledon on TV. We both like classical music. Pam has been patient to teach me about the masters and their music, and she has entered into my enthusiasm for birdwatching. In Waco we would often go to a window and take turns with the field glasses to watch a cardinal or a flicker or a woodpecker in a nearby tree.

Yet we are also distinctly different from each other. Pam likes cucumber sandwiches, mushrooms and blue cheese, which would not be my choice. She could live without baseball and football, which I enjoy. I am painfully slow to say what is on my mind, but Pam is seldom without a well-phrased answer. I seem to have a predisposition for making at least one wrong turn when driving an unfamiliar route, and forging ahead in the hope of finding my way. Pam, however, wants to stop and ask directions at the first inkling of confusion behind the wheel. These areas of difference could be fertile ground for squabbles.

"When you have disagreements, the only answer is prayer," a pastor's wife told us. Indeed, the knowledge that our daily prayer time is coming up spurs us to resolve any differences swiftly! Ken and Brenda Barker say they are thankful that they made prayer together a priority early in their marriage, for that daily appointment with God forces them to deal promptly with any problem. "If there is a rift between Brenda and me, some problem or difficulty that's unresolved, then we resolve it before we pray," Ken says. Thus the very existence of a shared prayer life forestalls what might otherwise escalate into full-blown conflict. Oliver Price of Dallas, writing in *Revival Insights,* tells us:

One time my wife, Betty, and I found ourselves dead-locked in opposite directions over a heart-wrenching decision. We prayed together about this. Neither of us tried to manipulate or pressure the other. We have prayed together enough to have complete freedom in talking to God in one another's presence. I listened to her pour out her heart and I poured out mine. Then we left the place of prayer understanding each other and sharing one another's feelings. We were confident that our Father would show us His will. After we waited patiently we both knew His will and did it.

7. The Door Prayer Opens into Intimacy

She writes . . .

Why should it be, I have often wondered, that we wives are more eager for spiritual intimacy than our husbands? Is it in the nature of men to be unself-disclosing concerning their feelings? Or do they wish they could be more open but don't know how to start?

At least one friend of mine believes that men simply do not have the same needs for intimacy that women have. She feels that Christian men tend to turn directly to God with their needs, often without expressing them to their wives, whereas wives want a spiritual openness not just with God but with their husbands. Other friends believe that many men would like to be able to reveal their inner-most selves, but were brought up at a time when the pre-vailing teaching was that males should keep their feelings under wraps.

Women, on the other hand, are usually able to express

their deep emotions to at least one other person. As I mentioned earlier, I came into a relationship with the living Lord Jesus when I was 21. It was to be 21 more years before I met Carey and entered into the kind of marriage relationship for which I had always longed.

During those years of singleness the Lord was very gracious to me. I may not always be able to say this—many committed Christians cannot say it—but I have always had the sense of His close presence. This was partly due to the fact that wherever I was in the world He gave me some very good women friends to be my prayer partners. I was able to tell my deepest feelings and needs to these women, and they in turn confided their needs to me. We prayed for each other accordingly and sensed God's closeness through our closeness to one another. I entered into marriage with prayer having been a vital part of the deepest relationships in my life and I certainly expected it to be a vital part of my marriage.

Many men have never experienced this kind of one-on-one sharing, and part of our loving and cherishing our husbands means that we must accept them as they are. One of the benefits of getting married later in life is a wide experience of human nature. My husband, for example, has a very responsible but lighthearted view of life. He laughs a lot and can be found on a cold and dark winter morning stepping outside on his way to work with a smile on his face and a clear "Good morning, world!" on his lips. I don't smile much on dark winter mornings. Life and getting to the office on time are very serious matters for me! Carey's attitude helps me a lot on such days.

Yet his same lighthearted view of life does not always have the same effect when we are trying to find an address somewhere in the Dallas metropolitan area where I am due to speak. Having grown up in Dallas, Carey usually assumes he knows exactly how to find the address of the meeting place. Dallas has undergone much structural change in the last fifty years, however. At the last moment we sometimes find we are not where we thought we were; after retracing our route and aiming the car in another direction we generally arrive not late, but later than I, with my over-meticulous forethought, would have preferred.

But I am learning that I cannot have it both ways! I love my husband deeply and I love what makes him what he is. He has a relaxed love relationship with life. He is not the worrier that I am. His strength in that area balances my weakness. His easygoing personality compensates again and again for my perfectionist tendencies. A byproduct of his lightheartedness is that he is not going to pore over maps for very long. I cannot change Carey's nature—and I don't want to. I must accept him as he is with all the byproducts of his strengths. That is part of my wedding vow to love and honor him.

As for our differing needs for spiritual intimacy, however, here I do not have the problem many wives have. Carey is wonderfully able to express his deepest thoughts and needs in our prayer together. He tells me, though, that this openness is a thing of recent years. It was only at the time that he lost his family through divorce that Carey began to allow a few trusted friends into the hidden places of his soul.

His experience has proved to me that although it is harder for men than for women to be vulnerable about their feelings, they can in time learn to be. I do not think that most Christian men are being deliberately obtuse. They simply do not recognize the extent to which their emotional lives are closed. Once they become aware of the deep desire for spiritual intimacy on the part of their wives, I believe that those men who are truly seeking God's best for their marriages will ask His help in tearing down the walls that block communication.

Prayer together as a couple is where the deepest spiritual intimacy is found. My first memory of prayer with Carey was three weeks after we met. I was preparing to leave for the airport to fly back to California when Carey and I prayed in the front room of the Waco home of my American "parents"—Charles and Dorothy Shellenberger. Sensing our need to be alone, Charles and Dorothy had conveniently left the house for a few minutes. Carey and I did not know each other well and there was a certain shyness between us as we joined hands and prayed in a general sense for each other's well-being. "Give him the desires of his heart, Lord," I remember praying for the man whom I had already grown to love.

During the next eight months we had many telephone conversations between Texas and California, usually in the evening after work. Each time, before we hung up, Carey gave me his blessing in the name of the Lord Jesus. This had a wonderfully calming effect on me as we awaited our wedding day and I knew I was being given a husband for whom prayer was very important.

Pastor C. W. Perry was to perform our wedding ceremony and he counseled me beforehand. "Make sure you pray together often," was his advice. "It is the best way to keep your relationship strong and close."

8. The Fellowship with God Created through Prayer

Has it happened in your life that an apparently chance remark someone made long ago on an ordinary day became engraved on your memory, being recalled again and again as experience proved the truth of it?

Probably having in mind the sheer difficulty and personal cost of his stand of faith that there were no closed doors to the Gospel, Brother Andrew, my boss at the time, remarked one day in the 1970s: "Perhaps this difficult work the Lord has given me was His only way of keeping me close to Him."

Those few words encouraged me many times in the years that followed. They had a way of helping me see things from God's point of view. Often when tempted to complain about the public and hectic way of life I shared with Corrie ten Boom during her traveling days, I thought of them. They came to mind later, too, during her years of illness and the confinement that was therefore also necessarily mine. *Perhaps,* I kept reminding myself, *the Lord has no other plan for bringing me into deeper fellowship with Himself than this particular thing that seems so difficult to me. I must therefore accept it.* And when I did, I had that peace that is the hallmark of being in the will of God.

After our marriage, the two years that Carey and I spent in Waco constituted the only extended time in my adult life that I did not have a daily job to go to. How I loved living in Waco! An oasis of quiet and peace, it seemed to me the ideal place in which to learn how to become a wife. What a gift the Lord gave me in those years!

During our second year there, as Carey has mentioned, I wrote *Safer Than a Known Way.* In it I traced the story of what happened after, as a 21-year-old in Sussex, England, I gave my life without reserve to the Lord Jesus. I recalled how I laid in His hands my three greatest fears: leaving England, having to speak in public and especially going through life unmarried. In the book I traced how during

the next 21 years the Lord fulfilled my life through the
very things I had feared. "Why is it that God can be trusted
with our lives?" the book asks. "Because only He knows the
way into the future He has planned for us." I remember
the satisfaction with which I completed the manuscript.
The Lord did indeed know the way. How glad I was that
He had led me to this oasis of a town and to my own little
house for the first time in my life! I was sure I would be
living in Waco happily ever after.

One day after I had sent the manuscript to the publisher, Carey called me from his office. Whereas a molehill
often looks like a mountain to me, Carey sees things much
more in their real proportions. It was therefore curious to
hear him say, "I want you to prepare yourself for some big
news." I braced myself. If Carey thought something was
big, I knew it must be. My husband proceeded to tell me
that his company had announced a corporate move from
out-of-the-way Waco to metropolitan Dallas. At first this
was difficult for me to accept. I did not want to leave our
quiet little town. But since I had just written *Safer Than a
Known Way,* the principles I had described were fresh in
my mind. Once more I remembered Brother Andrew's
words, "Perhaps this thing that God has allowed to happen
is His only way of bringing you closer to Himself."

From the outset we knew that the higher cost of living in
the Dallas area would make it necessary for me to work
outside the home. What kind of job could I find? Would
there be any way in which my unusual experience and
training of the past twenty years could be put to use? I did
not see how.

Then, a few weeks before we were to leave Waco, I
received a telephone call from a man I had known slightly
while he worked for Baylor University in Waco. Dr. Gary

Cook had recently been appointed president of Dallas Baptist University. He told me he wanted to start an intercessory prayer ministry at the university with the aim of turning every aspect of the school's life over to God. Having heard me speak one time, he knew that in the past I had worked for Christian leaders who knew how to pray and whose prayers had made a difference. Dr. Cook invited me to become director of Dallas Baptist University's new prayer ministry. I accepted the invitation with alacrity!

Carey and I moved to Grand Prairie, not far from the campus of the university, which is in the far southwest corner of the city. Keeping in mind that although I had the title of "director" of a prayer ministry I did not know more about prayer than many others, I found myself with the extraordinary privilege of seeking to encourage an increase in prayer on the campus. It was, and is, my daily task to ask as many as possible of our faculty, staff and students, "Does God really answer prayer? If He does, why are we not coming to Him more often; why are we as a Christian university not expecting much more from Him than we are now?"

As time progressed, we saw God honor Dr. Cook's desire to turn the life of the university increasingly over to Him. A prayer room in the quietest part of the campus, overlooking the nearby lake, was set aside and faculty, staff and students signed up to pray for the requests taken there daily. As word of the ministry spread, more and more requests not only from our campus but from near and wide outside it began to reach the intercessory prayer office. In addition, people began to confide to me requests that were for my ears only and which could not be shared with the other intercessors. I began to see that of all the works in the world, prayer may be the only one that is judged by God alone. He and only He knew whether or not I was being faithful in keeping my promises to pray. I knew that "He requires truth in the inward parts" and that we must not be a prayer ministry in name only.

Sometimes the needs of people weighed on me heavily. I began to wish I did not have to bear some of the burdens I was carrying in prayer. Then again I remembered those words from the past, "Perhaps this is God's only plan at this time for drawing you closer to Himself." If that was the case, what a privilege! I was being forced to pray as never before—and with each intercession, experiencing that fellowship with God that is the goal of our existence. Nor is my calling in any way unique. The very volume and load of the prayer requests coming to this one ministry shows me that the burden and privilege of intercessory prayer is meant to be shared by every Christian . . . and every Christian couple!

In this chapter we have tried to answer the question "*Why* should husbands and wives pray together?" Let's proceed now toward the *what, when* and *how.* In the next chapter we will introduce the basic stepping stones, as we see them, that lead to daily prayer together.

4
Foundations for Prayer

"Lord, teach us to pray."   Luke 11:1

He writes . . .

We are watching a new building take form on the campus of Dallas Baptist University. The new John G. Mahler Student Center is now an imposing structure of concrete and steel and brick, its roof nearing completion, its tall paneled windows already giving it something of a finished look.

When Pam and I first came to the campus the grassy knoll where this building now stands was barren and looked unpromising. A few months later a sign went up near the roadway, announcing this as the site of the new center. That was followed by months during which nothing much seemed to be happening. But all the while necessary preparations were being made. Workers were drilling through the unstable clay into the limestone bedrock, sinking reinforced concrete pillars to sustain the weight of the future structure.

In these early chapters we, too, are laying a foundation. For the workmen to hang the chandeliers and lay the carpets in the early days of construction would have been impossible. Likewise, we are eager to get quickly to the benefits of prayer together—the inspiring examples from other couples' experiences, encouragements and inducements to the life of prayer. But first, the foundation must be laid.

In the last chapter we enumerated some of the reasons husbands and wives should make a commitment to daily prayer. In a way, these were reasons from the human perspective. Now it seems right and necessary to look at prayer from God's vantage point, for in this conversation between God and man, He matters most. He makes prayer possible. He has set the ground rules. In this chapter, we will seek to identify a number of those ground rules—basic theological truths that lie at the base of a life of prayer. We cannot name them all, and in a sense we hesitate to name any, lest we find ourselves seeming to suggest that prayer consists of rules-keeping. Andrew Murray has rightly called it the "school of prayer," and only the ones who enroll there can know the lessons the Teacher is leading us into.

Forming what may be called a "theology of prayer," here are basic requisites as we see them:

1. Recognizing God's grace
2. Keeping faith in the Lord Jesus Christ
3. Walking in the light
4. Listening to the Spirit's voice
5. Loving all people
6. Resisting Satan
7. Surrendering to the will of God
8. Persevering to the end

In this book it is impossible to examine each of these foundational truths in detail, nor is that necessary since very much has been written about each one. Pam and I will attempt simply to define them one by one and emphasize how each relates to a fruitful, lifelong prayer life for couples.

1. Recognizing God's Grace

We believe that prayer was God's idea, so it seems good to start with this exquisite quality, God's grace. The New Testament is laced with this word through and through. John begins his Gospel: "The law was given through Moses; grace and truth were realized through Jesus Christ." Paul particularly loves this word, opening every one of his letters with some variation of this salutation: "Grace to you and peace from God our Father." In Romans, the most theological of his writings, he loves to dwell on God's grace: "We have peace with God through our Lord Jesus Christ, through whom we have gained access by faith *into this grace in which we now stand*" (Romans 5:1–2, NIV).

Whatever "grace" is, it broke open to all mankind with the coming of the Lord Jesus, and we who are Christians are knee-deep in it. Norman Snaith, writing in *A Theological Word Book of the Bible*, acknowledges that *grace* is essentially a New Testament word, but he sees its true origin in God's covenant-love to man. Even before the covenant with Israel existed, God revealed this attribute in his dealings with Noah, who "found grace [or favor] in the eyes of the Lord" (Genesis 6:8). "The connexion with the Old Testament use of the word 'grace' is to be found," says Snaith, "in the idea that God's favour is entirely free and wholly undeserved, and that there is no obligation of any kind that God should be favourable to his people."

These two truths seem to us especially relevant to the subject of prayer: We come to Him entirely undeserving and dependent upon His loving favor, and He is under no obligation at all to show us favor.

Even Christians can be heard today using the phrase "You deserve it!" when wanting to encourage someone. It is true that a secretary can "deserve" a raise, and a school-boy can "deserve" an *A* on his paper. But such thinking is dead wrong when the subject turns to what we receive from God. We don't have any ground to stand on with God. All religion, and even prayer, is rubbish and an abomination to God—unless there is in it the basic element of faith. And faith, or trust, involves acknowledging our bankruptcy in spirit. The Bible teaches that it is God's grace that enables us to admit our bankruptcy and repent, and it is His grace that provides us with the faith to come to Him. And yet we do have a vital part: We must choose to receive that grace. When we do, as Paul says, we are given access into "this grace in which we now stand."

A common description of *grace* is "unmerited favor." An even more concise definition is "Jesus Christ." Being "in Jesus Christ"—one of Paul's favorite expressions—is an-other way of saying "in grace." The husband and wife who are in Christ are favored; they have grace to stand before God and plead His mercy for anything or anyone upon their heart. I have deliberately used the singular *heart* here because the more a husband and wife pray together, the more their two hearts are united in one. The grace of God makes us worthy to pray with strong assurance that God hears and God answers.

2. Keeping Faith in the Lord Jesus Christ

The foundation stone of faith in Christ is so basic that we wonder if it needs stating. But some who are seeking the way to God can be confused. This should not surprise us, for in our "global village" every religion claims to be authentic. And religion inevitably teaches that "God" is approached through some work we do. One faith system alone insists that all work is worthless, save the finished work of Jesus Christ. The prayer that is the subject of this book is prayer offered by two who stand in God's grace and pray in the name of God's only Son.

"When the Son of Man comes," Jesus asked, "will he find faith on the earth?" (Luke 18:8). "Without faith," declares the writer of Hebrews, "it is impossible to please him, for he who comes to God must believe that he is, and that he is a rewarder of those who seek him" (11:6).

An important truth is here. Jesus did not say He was looking for *great* faith—only faith. If we think that prayer together is impossible because one or both of us has weak faith, then it may help to consider this: God asks only that we have faith. Weak faith in a strong God has wrought miracles before! And the way to more faith is to exercise the faith that we have.

Before we leave this point, an even more important truth seems in need of emphasis. In this book we are thinking of real prayer, of calling down answers from heaven, of making a difference in the world. But lest we think that *we* call the shots, we should look again at the subtitle above: Keeping Faith in the *Lord* Jesus Christ.

Jesus Christ, in whose name we pray, is the sovereign Lord of the cosmos. He is eternal and His "program" continues, while we come on the scene for a few years and then pass on. It is possible, we believe, to come to know Him in such a way as to cooperate with His purposes in the world—purposes that include our own little world of family and vocation and church and society, and purposes that encompass all mankind, "every kindred and people and tongue." He invited us to this cooperation in His model prayer, when He said: "This, then, is how you should pray:

'Our Father in heaven, hallowed be your name, your kingdom come, your will be done on earth as it is in heaven' "
(Matthew 6:9). For starters, the Lord's Prayer can lead us
to exercise faith in the Lord and Master and see Him bring
change and new beginnings, all because we pray. Declar-
ing that we have faith in the Lord Jesus is a simultaneous
admission of the soul's worship of the Lord, and of its
submission to Him.

To say it again: Faith in the Lord Jesus is required. Faith
is both the gateway into God's family and the way we travel
every day as His redeemed people.

3. Walking in the Light

To walk in faith is the Christian's victory. But that is so
much easier said than done. That is where this third truth
in our little theology of prayer comes in. As believers, we
love to dwell on the promises in the Bible that assure us of
answered prayer. Many of these promises appear in this
book. But they are not all of what God has to say concerning prayer. Now and again, both in the Old Testament and
the New, we encounter the hard truth that there are
prayers that God does not hear and therefore will not
answer. For example, in the book of Isaiah:

> "When you spread out your hands in prayer, I will
> hide my eyes from you; even if you offer many
> prayers, I will not listen. Your hands are full of blood;
> wash and make yourselves clean."   Isaiah 1:15–16

A holy God will not hear the prayers—even of His own
people—if the one praying is unclean. This is seen in the
Old Testament through the well-developed laws concern-

ing sacrifices for sin. The good news of the New Testament is that in turning one's back on sin and believing in Christ, all sin is forgiven and the new believer is declared "clean." But we know that none of us stays that way. We still sin. After we become Christians we are even more keenly aware of our sinfulness because our conscience is all awake to God and aware that He sees everything we do and everything we say—even our thoughts!

But the Gospel declares further that the possibility of a "new life" exists for us. It is the life of "walking in the light." John describes it in his first epistle:

> God is light; in him there is no darkness at all. If we claim to have fellowship with him yet walk in the darkness, we lie and do not live by the truth. But if we walk in the light, as he is in the light, we have fellowship with one another, and the blood of Jesus, his Son, purifies us from every sin. . . . If we confess our sins, he is faithful and just and will forgive us our sins and purify us from all unrighteousness.
>
> 1 John 1:5–7, 9

From these passages in Isaiah and in 1 John, we can clearly see that when we practice sin we lose God's listening ear. These Scriptures don't say we lose our stand in God's grace, but that we lose God's fellowship. This is much like a child who disobeys his parent. The parent may banish the child from his presence for an hour or so, but a good parent would never ban the child from the family. Sinning brings a cloud between us and the sunshine of God's favor. That sun still shines—He has not changed—we have just lost touch with Him for a while. I say "for a while," because presumably we will not want things to stay that way.

To walk in the light is to live with no unconfessed sin in our lives. We walk in the light by confessing any sin as soon as we become aware of it. Though we sin in thought or word or deed or something left undone or unsaid—and each of us does sin—we can, in a split second, tell God about it and be restored to the light. That is not to say that we will feel happy with ourselves. We may feel fairly miserable after confessing to God for the twentieth time in a day, but we have His Word that we are restored to the light as soon as we call on God. Our faith, that prerequisite, is in God's promised restoring, not in our feelings.

We may have been taught as children to say our prayers at bedtime, asking God to forgive us "if we have sinned." As a friend of mine would say, "That won't cut the mustard." Confessing sin is naming the specific fault before God. To confess is to say the same thing about a deed that God says about it. When I call some prideful act or word, for example, "sin," and admit it to God, I can trust Him to forgive it, for I have adopted the same attitude toward it that He has. We are in fellowship. We are walking in His light. And what is the use in waiting until bedtime for the blessing of God's presence?

Earlier we commented that none of us deserves an audience with God. He who is holy is quite apart from us. Yet there is a sense in which we can deserve God's ear and even His blessing. Pam and I do not dare make such a statement; it is a teaching of Scripture. The deserving is twofold: God has made us worthy by His grace, and we have "earned" a right to be heard because we have walked in the light He has given us.

First, it is not in ourselves but in Christ that the believer comes to God. We are "joint-heirs" with Christ, we are "accepted in the Beloved," and, incredible as it seems, we are "a fragrance of Christ to God" (2 Corinthians 2:15, NASB). When we are walking in fellowship, the fragrance of our lives, our sweet obedience, our thankfulness, our desire for the Father's glory—all of this reminds the Father of His Son and He *loves us as He loves His own Son.* No wonder the writer of Hebrews admonishes believers to come boldly before the throne of grace (Hebrews 4:16)!

Second, we "deserve" to be heard when we are walking in as much light as God has given to us. The plain reading of Scripture shows this to be true. God stipulates again and again the conditions for receiving answers to our prayers. Isaiah 58 is an example: "*Then* you will call, and the Lord will answer; you will cry for help, and he will say: Here am I" (verse 9).

Some may lift this verse from its context and claim that God thus binds Himself to answer anyone at any time. Yet, look again at this promise. If the Lord will answer *then,* we should ask *when* that is. The preceding verses indicate that God hears *when* we "remove the chains of oppression and the yoke of injustice, and let the oppressed go free. Share your food with the hungry and open your homes to the homeless poor. Give clothes to those who have nothing to wear, and do not refuse to help your own relatives" (verses 6–7, TEV). In its entirety the passage promises that God will answer prayer when we stop being critical ("pointing the finger"), when we quit dirty, abusive speech, when we give ourselves to the hungry and satisfy the desire of the afflicted.

Most of us would disqualify ourselves from any notion of deserving God's blessing based on this one passage that describes the sort of unselfish living He expects from us. But these are not unrealistic requirements. If we do our

best and confess to Him where we fall short, we can confidently expect our prayers to be heard.

For most of us, it takes years to reach the point where we
are assured of God's forgiveness on a moment-by-moment
basis. If maintaining this unbroken fellowship is quite a
trick for an individual, imagine what complexities enter
the picture when two people attempt to walk in the light
with one another as well as with God. But that is the incredible ideal set forth in God's Word.

When I was a young Christian I heard more mature
Christians talk about "keeping short accounts." I am no
accountant, but I believe that the term refers to a banking
practice. I suppose that an early banker, knowing that
some governing body would regulate the bank and peri-
odically inspect and audit it, soon learned to keep track of
every penny on a daily basis—or else the numerous trans-
actions on subsequent days would lead to chaos when the
authorities called for a reckoning. In marriage, this "short-
accounts" principle is equally necessary. Prayer as a couple
cannot thrive without it.

I can well remember a day when keeping short accounts
prevented my ruining a memorable occasion. It was Christmas Day 1990, a day that had been perfect up until the
point where I messed up. My beloved Pam had prepared
a sumptuous Christmas dinner—turkey with all the trim-
mings. Joining us and Jim were her father, who had come
from California as is his custom at Christmastime, and
"Honey," my ninety-year-old stepmother, whom we had
collected from her retirement home in East Dallas. The
meal ended with hot plum pudding, after which we all
retired to the back room to watch "The Nutcracker" on
television.

It was dark as I helped Honey into the front seat of the

car while Pam and Dad climbed into the back for the ride
to Honey's residence. I had to borrow Pam's car keys, having left mine in the house—an oversight that should have
alerted me to consider what else I had overlooked. But I
was still savoring our "perfect day."

Our plan was to detour enroute in order to view the
Dallas Christmas lights, so we drove away with still more
expectations after a rich—in more ways than one!—afternoon together.

As I approached the first traffic signal on the parkway I
suddenly realized that my wallet and driver's license were
back at the house. We were a hundred feet from the in-
tersection when the light changed to yellow. *Better not drive
all the way across Dallas and back without a license,* my mental
process ran.

The light turned a solid red, but I made no attempt to
brake. Intent on finding a place to turn around I scanned
the crossing and, without touching the brake pedal, proceeded through the red light and moved into the left lane.

Simultaneously from the back seat came two excited
voices: "Stop! Stop!"

What could I say? How I wished I were alone, and that
no one had witnessed what I had just done! The defiant
thought followed swiftly: *You didn't do anything so bad.*
Sheepishly I explained, "We have to go back. I left my
wallet at the house." But Pam persisted, "Why did you run
the light? You could have got us killed."

She was right, of course. It was very careless of me.
From the back seat Pam asked if I was all right. I wished
only that she would be quiet. We returned to the house
with me muttering, "I'm sorry. I'm O.K. I just realized I
don't have my driver's license and I was momentarily confused."

When I reached our driveway, Pam got out of the car, too. Then, adding insult to injury, she asked if she should drive. I stifled my emotions and hurried upstairs in search of the wallet. To make matters worse, it wasn't where I "knew" it would be. Frustration mounted. Pam said nothing more, but waited quietly downstairs. At last I located the wallet and assumed a confident air as I again faced my wife at the door. Her eyes questioned me and, trying to smooth over my transgression, I shrugged and soon was driving—cautiously—down the parkway again.

Pam said nothing more, but even from the back seat I could feel the icy distance between us. I knew what I had to do.

Pulling the car to the side of the road and turning to my three passengers, I confessed the bad driving and asked forgiveness of them. I then asked meekly if anyone still wanted to see the Christmas lights. All three assured me they did, the signal that told me the relationship had been restored.

Had I continued walking in darkness rather than in the light, I could have spoiled the balance of the day for all four of us. And had Pam and I not talked out any residue of feeling on both our parts before going to bed, we surely could not have prayed then, or begun the following day with any assurance of God's blessing.

If marriage can be thought of in that metaphor of "walking together," and if agreeing together is basic to that walk, then some mechanism needs to be in place whereby the couple maintain their agreement. Some means is needed that allows—even insists on—keeping short accounts. Communication is, of course, that method. Having a daily tryst, a regular meeting time and place for the couple to draw apart together, opens wide the door to communication, and is one of the reasons we are so grateful for the rhythm of daily prayer.

4. Listening to the Voice of the Spirit

> Master, speak, Thy servant heareth
> Longing for Thy gracious word.
> Longing for the voice that cheereth,
> Master, let it now be heard.
> I am listening, Lord, to Thee.
> Master, speak, O speak to me.
> Frances Ridley Havergal (1836–1879)

She writes . . .

Of all the children in the Bible, Samuel was the one whose example the Lord held before me when I was a self-centered little girl. I had a grudging admiration for young Samuel who, on hearing the voice of the Lord in the Temple, said: "Speak, Lord, for Your servant is listening." I had not yet called my Savior "Lord," and I certainly did not want to hear what He might say. Then I might have to obey and obedience would probably be costly! Since 1965, however, I have called Jesus Christ "Lord" and more than anything I want to learn to listen to His voice.

"What is prayer? What is your favorite definition?" I asked a group of D.B.U. students recently when Dr. David Fletcher invited me to speak on prayer in his Christian living class. "It is talking to God," said a student named Paul. "And listening to Him." I liked Paul's definition, especially the last part. Very often our concept of prayer involves talking to God, forgetting that listening is the essential second half of communication.

In the Old Testament, before the Holy Spirit was given, God spoke in an audible voice to His servants the prophets who then reported to the people the word of the Lord. But we live after Pentecost, and to us is given the priceless gift of the indwelling Holy Spirit. We can know God in a different way than did His Old Testament people. Actually hearing the voice of God speaking audibly is rare in our times; instead we can learn to discern the voice of the Holy Spirit in our hearts and minds. In this book we are talking about prayer as couples, but before we can hear His voice as a couple, we need to have learned to hear it individually.

Not every Christian can hear the voice of the Holy Spirit. That voice, I believe, can be heard only by those who have become like the child Samuel. His relationship to God was that of a servant to his Lord. On a weekend in March 1965, when I called Jesus Christ "Lord" for the first time and asked Him to speak to me, I heard His voice. It was not an audible voice, but it was just as unmistakable. Throughout my being I received the assurance that God had heard my prayer, and in the years since He has spoken to me often in this manner. I have frequently found my naturally shy personality a drawback, but when it comes to communion with the Lord it is perhaps an asset, for I love solitude and silence. I seek it. When I am alone I rarely turn on a radio or television since quietness is one of my greatest joys.

When I worked for Brother Andrew in The Netherlands, I rented two small rooms on the second floor of a private house in the town of Harderwijk. It was there that I began to learn to listen to God. At first I knew few people and did not speak Dutch. Lacking these human contacts I was able to spend many hours alone with God. I sought to be quiet before Him, to concentrate on Him and to hear His voice.

"Be still and know that I am God" is a verse from the Psalms that often echoes wistfully through my mind in these much busier days when solitude seems hard to come by. Sometimes people tell me, "God does not speak to me." Could it be that you and I often do not create the quiet circumstances wherein the Holy Spirit, who speaks very softly, can be heard? God cannot usually get through to us in noise and bustle and confusion. His is a still, small voice. And in order to hear it we must not only cultivate a quiet spirit, but work hard to find a quiet place in which to listen.

After I had worked seven years for Brother Andrew, somebody approached me one day with the news that Corrie ten Boom's companion was to be married shortly and that Tante Corrie needed a new companion. "How about you?" my friend said with typical Dutch bluntness. "You know the language and the culture, you are not married and would therefore be free to help her."

"Not I," I replied quickly. "I am not the companion type." I hoped to leave the matter there, but the Lord reminded me in the ensuing days of my promise made years before in England to serve Him wherever He should send me. I decided that I would take Sunday afternoon, when I knew I could rely on having a few quiet hours, to seek God's will.

On an early spring day, then, in 1976, I set aside my Sunday afternoon and as far as I was able, sought God's will for my future. It was very simple really. I just put into His hands again all my life. I surrendered to Him my love for Harderwijk, the friends I had made there and especially the exciting work with which I had been involved for more than seven years. I gave it all back to Him, and said, "Lord, if you wish me to leave Holland and help Corrie ten Boom on her world travels for a little while, I am willing." A couple of hours later the telephone rang, my first phone call of the day. It was Corrie ten Boom's companion to tell me that during her prayer time that afternoon Tante Corrie had come to believe she should approach me about the possibility of my working with her. God the Holy Spirit spoke to me through the coinciding of her prayers that day with mine. The Holy Spirit speaks in normal, unspectacular ways, but when He does there is no mistaking His voice.

Years later, when Corrie ten Boom was silenced through a stroke, I could see a little more clearly the wisdom of God in asking me, who loves silence, to be one of those who watched and waited with her. I have to confess that I had even more silence during those years than I enjoyed, but I also had the opportunity to practice hearing the voice of the Holy Spirit in the hours and hours of quietness in the front bedroom of Tante Corrie's house in California. I came to know without a doubt that surrender to God's will and silence are the vital factors in hearing the voice of the Holy Spirit.

Carey and I want to learn to hear the voice of the Holy Spirit together. We are discovering that He will often give each of us the same message when we pray in surrender and in quietness. One of the joys of couple prayer is the assurance this experience gives. Usually He speaks to us in very ordinary ways, such as yesterday when we both, after prayer, came up with the identical sum of money we believed He would have us send to somebody.

Other times the Holy Spirit speaks to just one of us. One of the challenges and joys of marriage for me is learning to respect Carey more and more. When a matter is not clear to me and is to him, I am learning to follow his lead. God gives me peace when I follow Carey's leading as surely as if I had heard His voice myself. Last evening is a case in point. I dislike shopping and spend as little time as possible in stores. Partly for this reason, for years I have avoided buying a winter coat. Who needs a winter coat in Texas, I ask myself, when it will be cold for an average of seven days a year?

My husband had been telling me for several months, however, that he wanted me to have a winter coat this year and was not to be put off by my protestations that this is a waste of money. I began to see that now that I am married I must listen to my husband through whom the Holy Spirit will speak to me in such a small matter as a coat and in larger matters, too. After a trip to the mall last evening I am now the contented owner of the most beautiful coat I have ever possessed, and certainly the first bright red one! Perhaps there is a cold winter ahead, but certainly there are much bigger decisions awaiting us, decisions when I will need to hear the voice of the Lord through the godly man God has given me as my husband. As I listen to his daily prayers, I am learning to respect him even more.

> O give me Samuel's ear
> The open ear, O Lord.
> Alive and quick to hear each whisper of Thy word.
> Like him to answer at Thy call
> And to obey Thee first of all.
> James D. Burns (1823–1864)

5. Loving All People

He writes . . .

As Pam and I have already observed, God would not be God apart from grace. He would also not be God without love. "God is love," John states succinctly. In the revelation of God throughout the Bible, this characteristic of love is a theme of every writer. Our world's pain and evil may cloud our vision, but the truth shines on: "God so loved the world. . . ." Jesus, when asked to name the greatest commandment, reaffirmed unhesitatingly that we are to love God with the whole heart, and soul, and strength, and our neighbor as ourselves—sending His listeners back to the ancient book of Leviticus (19:18) as proof that the commandment of love-without-exception is a basic, abiding, God-given requirement.

When the Lord Jesus spent His last evening in the presence of the twelve disciples, He gave them the watchword of the new community of God: *Love one another.* "By this," He added, "all men will know that you are My disciples, if you have love for one another" (John 13:35, NASB).

Paul caught this truth and lived by it. To the Corinthian believers this once-rigid religious Pharisee wrote, "For the love of Christ constrains us" (2 Corinthians 5:14, KJV). So irresistible had Paul learned this love to be that he used the word translated "constrain," which elsewhere in the New Testament speaks of a disease that invades a person. Writing to those same Corinthians, he paused to try to define love, and said:

> Love is patient and kind; love is not jealous or boastful; it is not arrogant or rude. Love does not insist on its own way; it is not irritable or resentful; it does not rejoice at wrong, but rejoices in the right. Love bears all things, believes all things, hopes all things, endures all things. . . . So faith, hope, love abide, these three; but the greatest of these is love.
>
> 1 Corinthians 13:4–7, 13, RSV

Being constrained by Christ's love, Paul prayed for every church about which he had any knowledge. He prayed for the specific needs of individuals by name, and he asked that the love of those for whom he prayed would grow. "May the Lord make your love increase and overflow for each other and for everyone else, just as ours does for you" (1 Thessalonians 3:12).

As John particularly wrote about the source of love— "We love because he first loved us" (1 John 4:19)—Paul constantly instructed the Church to love all mankind.

What is it that causes you to pray for your wife or husband? For your child? For your best friend, and all for whom you pray regularly? Love, you would say. Truly, "love bears all things" and keeps praying. This is why love is necessary to any theology of prayer: It is the energizing force that drives us ever to seek God and His blessing for the beloved.

Paul wanted the Thessalonians to abound in love, however, not only for one another, but "for all men." This suggests what to do when we realize that we don't love someone in particular. Love, which can empower our prayer life, is from God. I admit, however, that I don't love lots of people. But God does, and all that is necessary is to say, "Father, I'm willing to love ____. I don't even want to love him/her, but I thank You that You can help me be willing, and love through me. Let Your love flow out through me to this person until I cannot know whether the love I feel for him/her is Your love or mine."

"Do you find praying for the five billion souls on planet earth a burden?" When someone put that question to me, I scanned his face for a smile that would denote he was teasing. Loving me and mine was all I could handle! And here was someone assuming I could love the whole world. Well, no, he assumed I *prayed* for the world. As Christians, you and I cannot close our hearts and minds—or our prayers and our love—to anyone. Christ has sent us into "the world." We ought to feel, as we grow in Christ, a growing burden for all people. God's love for all people will lead us to look ever more lovingly on others. And while we will feel the burden, and it will become intense and nearly unbearable at times, we must recognize that we are not to carry that burden ourselves. We cannot. It will crush us.

Perhaps we should begin this assignment of loving all people by asking God to help us love the people in our families, our churches and our everyday spheres of activity. Pam and I have found that it helps to record the names of individuals in this "world" of ours, and to assign them a day in our prayer notebook, so that on that day we can love them through prayer. We will talk more about this prayer list in chapter 7, and suggest ways to expand our praying until we are interceding, in a responsible way, for groups and entire nations.

From those who have walked with the Lord in deeper fellowship than we, Pam and I have learned the further truth that God's indwelling love, which is a fruit of His indwelling Spirit, is the source of strength for praying. His love turns the duty of intercession into joy and purposeful conversation with the Father, and when we see His answers to our feeble, weak praying, we find new energy for continuing the work of prayer.

6. Resisting Satan

> Restraining prayer we cease to fight
> Prayer makes the Christian's armour bright.
> And Satan trembles when he sees
> The weakest saint upon his knees.
> William Cowper (1731–1800)

She writes . . .

As we said at the outset, Carey and I believe that the chief aim of Christian couples in praying together should be coming to know God. By this we do not mean knowing about Him, or even knowing that He is vitally interested in the large and small details of our lives, but actually knowing Him in the sense of knowing His heart, coming into His presence, discovering what His will is and seeking to align our lives with His will.

Carey used Job as an example of a man whose passionate prayer resulted in knowing God. One of the oldest books of the Bible and mysteriously antique to me, the book of Job tells us of a man with whom many of us who have gone through grief can identify. Not a few of us have known deep and tragic losses. "You must feel like Job" are sometimes the only words I can find when, in my office at the university, people confide to me for prayer details of profoundly difficult personal circumstances.

From our privileged place in time, however, we know something that Job did not know. Job was not aware that his misfortunes resulted from the malice of Satan. We have no excuse for not knowing about the enemy. We have the New Testament, which warns us to be on the alert for the devious antics of the devil. Like a strong and vicious lion, Peter tells us, he is seeking to encircle unwary prey (1 Peter 5:8–9).

What Satan fears more than anything is prayer. He knows that prayer unleashes the power of God. Because Jesus overcame Satan once and for all on the cross, you and I can exercise our dearly bought right of access in prayer to the Father. And when a Christian couple asks Him, "Father, show us what You are doing in our day and help us align ourselves with Your purposes," Satan will employ all his time-worn tactics to disrupt their prayer life.

What are the tactics of Satan? They are the kinds of ploys one would expect from somebody of his character. Among other things, the Bible tells us that he is a murderer, a destroyer and a liar. Satan knows that God has ordained prayer as the way His purposes are accomplished and he knows his time is short. He will therefore throw as many obstacles as he can muster into the path of the Christian's prayer. Unless the believer is watchful, he or she may be tempted to believe the lie continually whispered by the enemy that prayer is an option rather than a necessity, that it involves time that could be spent more profitably in some other way or that the prayers of ordinary people don't make much difference.

Recently we were worshiping in a church where the Bible teacher Iverna Tompkins was speaking. She asked her audience, "How much authority does Satan have in your life?" and then provided the answer, "As much as you allow him." To the degree that we accept his lies in the views set before us in society—materialistic values and moral compromise—we are allowing the devil authority that is rightfully the Lord's.

"Resist Satan," says the Lord in 1 Peter 5:9. How is that effected? First, we must be aware that he is a very real enemy. Second, we must know that we have nothing to fear from him for he is a completely defeated foe. Third, we must follow the example of the Lord Jesus and counter Satan's devilish whispered lies with the truth of Scripture. "It is written, it is written, it is written," said the Lord Jesus in Matthew 4. Then, the Gospel continues, the devil left Him.

In our prayers it is not unusual for one of us to tell the

Father that we are resisting the devil in the particular matter about which we are praying. At times we even speak directly to the devil: "Satan, we resist you in the name of the Lord Jesus Christ; you must get your hands off Tommy" (or whomever we are interceding for). In praying for those regions of the earth where spiritual darkness is long-standing, we ask the Father by His mighty Spirit to push back the darkness: "Make these lands Your lands, Lord. We proclaim that Jesus is Victor."

I try to make a deliberate daily effort to "put on the Lord Jesus Christ," claiming my invincible position in Him. Reciting Ephesians 6:10–18, I put on the whole armor of God, piece by piece, reminding myself and the devil of verse 11, that when I am fully clad in the armor of God I "can take [my] stand against the devil's schemes."

When Carey and I come to our daily prayer time together, we frequently have to deal with the devil early in the session. We believe our prayer time to be our evening's most important work, yet we are often tempted not to pray, but rather to rest and read the newspaper or return telephone calls or open the mail. Often we find a curious tiredness comes over us, or a feeling of unworthiness. These, we are coming to recognize, are some of the tactics of the liar who delights in Christians' failure to pray. But the lies can be easily countered by "resisting him, strong in faith" at the beginning of our prayer time. Tiredness and unworthiness disappear when the name of the Lord Jesus is brought to bear on the situation, and we enter prayer with the knowledge that through Him we are indeed strong.

Binding Satan is a term from Jesus' own teaching, recorded both in Matthew 12 and Mark 3. Here Jesus has been accused of casting out demons by the power of Satan, being somehow in league with the devil. "How can Satan drive out Satan?" He asks (Mark 3:23), and goes on to declare that a kingdom (Satan's) divided against itself cannot stand. Then come these words: "No one can enter the strong man's house and plunder his property unless he first binds the strong man, and then he will plunder his house" (verse 27, NASB).

The "strong man" here, of course, is the devil. Jesus does give this to Satan: He is strong. But he is no match for the Lord Jesus. Jesus has "bound" Satan and is exorcising demons left and right. In so doing, He is plundering the devil's "house."

Today in America, just the reverse is happening. Satan is plundering God's house. In Europe he has already well nigh decimated the whole spiritual edifice so that in parts of the continent God's house seems hardly to exist. But there are hopeful signs as God awakens and stirs many of His people in the United Kingdom and elsewhere. For the last two years, in Eastern Europe and the former Soviet Union, the Gospel has been running across the "strong man's" domain with abandon, children are again being taught about God, the Bible is being read everywhere and even preached in assembly halls that once were Communist Party strongholds. What happened?

The Church—both the "suffering Church" within those former Soviet bloc countries and the Church in the West—prayed down the strong man's walls and bound his power, and Jesus showed Himself indeed to be "the light that shines through the darkness—and the darkness can never extinguish it" (John 1:5, TLB).

Here and there in America and Great Britain and all over the world are those who, like the first-century Christians to whom Paul wrote, are "not ignorant of Satan's devices." Carey and I have never known so many churches to form intercessory prayer ministries as we see doing so now. Teaching concerning spiritual warfare is on the increase in many churches. But the strong "walls" of crime and violence and drug addiction and sexual perversion and political and corporate corruption will not give way unless Christians unite to bind the devil. The offensive can begin in a given location with a single couple in the intimacy of their own relationship and the shelter of their own home. Imagine what would happen if every believing couple in your community bound the devil in their prayers consistently. Binding the devil is our work of resisting Satan, and it is done by proclaiming that Jesus Christ is Lord—for our children, for our church leaders, for those in authority, for any who are harassed by demonic forces. "In all these things we are more than conquerors through him who loved us" (Romans 8:37).

7. Surrendering to the Will of God

He writes . . .

Dear friends sat with Pam and me in the cozy back room of our house. Gail and Dennis Linam, parents of three grown children, were looking back on a richly blessed marriage and telling us how prayer had been their strength and is their strength now even more.

"There has never been a time in our marriage when we did not pray," says Gail, "but like most who choose to be true disciples, we have known sorrow and testings that have brought forth prayers of anguish." One of those times was when their oldest daughter became critically ill with ravaging juvenile rheumatoid arthritis, which attacked the linings of her lungs and racked her body with unbearable pain.

At one point in Angela's illness, Gail was at their daughter's bedside in a hospital in Houston, and Dennis was on his knees back home in Waco. "I can't describe the agony we were going through," recalls Dennis. "That night I felt we might lose our seventeen-year-old Angela. We were trusting the Lord, but it appeared we were losing the battle. I don't know how long I prayed, but I reached the point of surrender, where I relinquished her to the Lord. I've never known such a struggle in all my life, because I could not understand God's will. But He must have given grace to relinquish her and her life and our own will to Him. And when I gave her up a great peace came over me. . . ."

In a truly miraculous way several weeks later, God acted. Angela's lungs stabilized. She could walk again. Dennis and Gail received their daughter back joyfully and she soon returned home. Angela made a steady recovery and is alive today, a beautiful brown-haired young woman with a professional degree, and happily married. While the disease remains, through prayer Angela faces each day confidently.

"True prayer," says John Stott, "is a variation on the theme 'Thy will be done.'" What Dennis and Gail experienced is asked of each of us who would follow Christ—the yielding of our wills to God. Earlier we noted that effective prayer for couples begins with acknowledging the Lordship of Jesus Christ. This yielding of the will is where the rather abstract concept of Lordship becomes very practical and concrete.

Jesus set the pattern when He prayed, "Not My will, but

Yours be done." Ed Byers, writing in the National Prayer Corps *Newsletter*, says:

> Yielding of self is the quality we need in our praying. Jesus [taught] us the secret to answered prayer. . . . Jesus withdraws any suggestion of [His own] plan, and accepts the will of His Father. That is the key to the victory, not only for Jesus but for all of us. Every believer has the victory over sin and death because Jesus yielded to the Father's will. That is the key to the victory in prayer also. Being in the Father's will is the positive assurance that prayer will be answered.

It is a mystery beyond explaining that we approach God's throne with definite things we desire, and God listens, having a will in these matters, too. We can make two mistakes at this point. One is to assume that our will is God's will. We adopt the attitude "My mind is made up; don't confuse me with the facts"—the fact being that God may have a better idea than what we are asking for.

A second mistaken attitude is a sort of fatalism that prays: "Please heal Aunt Martha of her arthritis, but Your will be done." This hands-off approach is not what Jesus modeled in the Garden. He did not glibly turn over His concern about the impending crucifixion, and the suffering and humiliation involved, by recalling a stanza of "Have Thine Own Way, Lord" and reciting it in a passionless manner. No, He wrestled. He agonized on His face. He sweat drops of blood. Accepting the Father's will was killing Him, and He fought for His life. But He let go of His own way and embraced the Father's will.

One error in Muslim thinking—and praying—is this fatalistic outlook. One follower of Islam excused his careless, reckless driving on mountain roads in Turkey because of a blind belief that if he met with an accident it was the will of Allah! The Christian rather is called to find out what God's will is (Colossians 1:9), and, having discovered it, to lay down his or her own will and act accordingly.

Accepting God's will does not always involve such a struggle, but it often does. When the struggle continues with no apparent breakthrough, God may be doing a number of things. He is seeing if the prayers from our lips rise from hearts that are earnest and single-minded. He is, no doubt, looking for faith that honors Him. And it could be that He is bringing us around to seek not only the thing for which we are pleading, but much more. Often He desires that we see the bigger picture, that we look on things more and more from His viewpoint.

Protracted praying has the effect upon us of bringing us to know Him—which Pam and I have defined as the meaning of prayer. And as we come to know Him better, we come to trust Him more.

Are you wrestling with God in a matter right now? Is there an "Isaac" in your life that God is asking you to place on the altar? The sooner you say to the Father—and mean—"Your will be done," the sooner you will come to rest and peace. In her book *Safer Than a Known Way,* Pam tells of the peace she was given following her prayer of relinquishment. Tranquility filled her, assuring her that

> beyond all doubt my future was perfectly safe with Him. But the strongest confirmation of the presence of God was His love. It was as if I were in a sea full of love. Wave upon wave of love broke over my head, strong and irresistible. It had a holy quality and grew

so intense that I had to pray, "Lord God, please stop
it. Please save some of this for heaven."

These then are the "ground rules" for a life of prayer as
husbands and wives: recognizing the grace of God, keeping faith in Christ, walking in the light, listening to the
Spirit, loving all people, binding Satan, surrendering to
God, and one more.

8. Persevering to the End

You will undoubtedly agree with Pam and me that there
is a paradox here: Prayer gives rest to the soul—yet at the
same time it is wearisome work. The Christian is called to
this toil every day, for all of life. All the more reason for
sharing the work with a prayer partner!

Perseverance, according to the dictionary, is "steady persistence in a course of action." It is "doggedness," "stead-
fastness," "tenacity," a "resolute and unyielding holding
on."

Every achiever recognizes the value of perseverance.
President Calvin Coolidge once said: "Press on. Nothing in
the world can take the place of persistence. Talent will not:
nothing is more common than unrewarded talent. Education alone will not: the world is full of educated failures.
Persistence alone is omnipotent."

The word translated "perseverance" in the King James
Version of the Bible appears only once, and that one instance has to do with intercessory prayer: "Praying always
with all prayer and supplication in the Spirit, and watching
thereunto with all perseverance and supplication for all
saints" (Ephesians 6:18). The various versions shed more
light on this quality in prayer: "Keeping alert and persis-

tent as you pray for all Christ's men and women" (J. B. Phillips edition). "Never get tired of staying awake to pray for all God's holy people" (The Jerusalem Bible). "Keep praying earnestly for all Christians everywhere" (The Living Bible).

To persevere in prayer seems possible only as we do it daily. In our urban society we live too far apart to come together daily in a local church as Christians used to. Countless individuals persevere alone in daily prayer, but it is a very good thing to have someone alongside, shouldering the burden with you. "Pity the man who falls and has no one to help him up" (Ecclesiastes 4:10).

Many objects of our praying require perseverance. And I know all too well how discouraging this can be. After the breakup of my marriage, prayer became a way of life for me. And because I usually prayed alone, I was often disheartened.

In December 1984, my son Jon, on Navy leave, joined me for a day of sightseeing in New York. First we toured the carrier *Intrepid,* and then we took the subway to the World Trade Center. Reaching the gleaming twin towers we joined the elevator queue for the observation deck. Height usually does not affect my digestive system. But that day we had gulped down a quick lunch and I recall feeling sick as we rose 110 floors above the ground. What was really upsetting me, I knew, was the stubborn invisible wall between my son and me.

Jon and I were not close at the time, and as we had shared the day I felt a tremendous longing for something that I could not quite put my finger on. I wanted intimacy with Jon, to be allowed into his world. I am sure that I was also yearning for our whole family to be together again with no walls between any of us.

The elevator doors opened and we two, with a throng of other sightseers, walked onto the expansive observation deck. We soon separated, each following where his own curiosity led him, amazed at the view that stretched out beyond the windows in all directions. From the nearest window I looked down on the Hudson River and New Jersey beyond it. From the next I could see southward past the Statue of Liberty to the Verrazano-Narrows Bridge.

I stopped, transfixed. People came and went, but for a long while—it must have been ten minutes—I seemed all alone as I studied the scene in the harbor. A few large ships, mostly freighters, were making their way in or out of the docking area. But further out, here and there as if parked, were other large vessels, sitting motionless in the water, apparently waiting until an assigned pier became vacant and ready for them and their cargo.

Suddenly it was as though God lifted back the curtain that veiled my own world. The sight of the motionless ships served as a parable for me. For I felt sure that just as each vessel would in time find its destined berth, my prayers too would come home. God seemed to whisper to me, *See, My son, those ships cannot move now, for the way isn't prepared for them yet. But in a matter of time, each will come into port. And it's that way with what you are praying for. Be patient. At the right time, when all is ready, your ship will come in too.* This unexpected revelation served to greatly encourage me to persevere in prayer for the family.

Almost a year later one of my ships did come in, when Jon, on duty at sea in the Pacific, wrote asking forgiveness for his attitude toward me and wanting our relationship restored. I read and reread that letter, so grateful that I had not quit praying. Since then Jon has underscored his intention in many ways, even honoring me this year with the privilege of snapping his ensign bars on his dress uniform as he was commissioned in a university ceremony as a U.S. Navy officer. Whenever I feel anxious about waiting for a prayer to be answered, I think of our visit to the World Trade Center. When I understand that the delay is for some purpose, I can go on persevering in prayer, believing and hoping.

Pam has told me about a Scripture plaque that hung on the wall in Corrie ten Boom's bedroom. The Scripture was from Psalm 31:15: "My times are in your hands." Those words had been of comfort to Corrie, and to Pam and her helpers during the prolonged illness. And to me they sum up what I realized that day with Jon at the World Trade Center. The years since then have only proved that God's timing is never a moment too soon or too late. But how many of us miss this lesson because we give up our praying?

> More things are wrought by prayer
> Than this world dreams of. Wherefore, let thy voice
> Rise like a fountain for me night and day.
> For what are men better than sheep or goats
> That nourish a blind life within the brain,
> If, knowing God, they lift not hands of prayer
> Both for themselves and those who call them friends?
> For so the whole round earth is every way
> Bound by gold chains about the feet of God.
>   Alfred, Lord Tennyson (1809–1892)

5

The Big Hurdle: "If We Are Willing"

"Teach me to do your will, for you are my God."
Psalm 143:10

He writes . . .

Pam reminded me recently of a difficult time in her life.
It was in the autumn of 1983. She had been at Corrie's
bedside in April as she died, and had gone about the numerous tasks that accompanied closing their home there in
Placentia, California. At last she boarded a plane for England, eager to return to her family in Hastings after being
away six years—only to find her mother waiting for her at
the London airport in a wheelchair. She had known that a
bone disease had been diagnosed in her mother's leg, but
not that it had progressed so far.

In her book *Safer Than a Known Way*, Pam described her
reaction:

> As Dad began the two-hour journey through the
> Sussex countryside to Hastings my heart began to
> sink. Was it possible that having been through a ter-
> minal illness with Tante Corrie I was facing the same
> thing so soon with my mother?
>
> When we arrived at their little house on the cliffs

overlooking the Channel I could see that Mother's painful leg was incapacitating her severely. She received me into their home with her usual loving hospitality, however, even struggling upstairs because she wanted to see my face when I viewed the front bedroom she and Dad had had newly decorated for me. I admired the new carpeting and the fresh wallpaper with its green and white pattern, but the thing to which my eye was mainly drawn was a rectangular card propped up on the mantlepiece. Eleven words were written in varying shades of green, colored with a child's hand. It was a card of welcome for me from Naomi, my sister's nine-year-old daughter. The words were from Psalm 143: "Teach me to do your will, for you are my God."

That night as I lay in bed, light from the streetlamps allowed me to make out those eleven words. I read and reread them and it was as if the Lord asked me to make another surrender of my will to Him. . . .

True enough, as Pam settled into her parents' home, she discovered that God's will for her was to help her dad take care of her mother until her death that December. Weary from the five-year illness of Corrie ten Boom, Pam says she could not have found strength to care for her dying mother without the daily repetition of those words, "Teach me to do your will." Now another autumn has come around, and Pam and I are yoked together in this book, which we believe is as needed by the Church as Pam was needed that autumn of 1983 by her mother and dad. In this chapter, we will be describing the "big hurdle" some of you face as you begin praying together as husbands and wives. The "big hurdle," as Pam and I have chosen to call it, is being willing.

We believe that God not only teaches us to do His will, He helps us clear the hurdle; He helps us to be willing. It is God, Paul tells us, who is "at work in you, both *to will* and to work for His good pleasure" (Philippians 2:13, NASB). If we are not yet willing to set aside "prime time" each day for prayer as a couple, we can at least pray, "Father, we're willing . . . to be willing. We're not willing now, but please help us want to be willing."

Nor should we wait for some feeling to arise from within, some emotion to tell us that now at last we are in the mood. The last half of Naomi's verse is as important as the first: *for you are my God.* Couples who have been praying together many years have confided that they do not always *feel* like praying when the time arrives. We experience that also. As we said earlier, we frequently feel fatigued, or discouraged, or pressed for time. That is when we need to remind ourselves of the old illustration of the locomotive and the train. The engine pulls the train, not vice-versa. If our feelings are in the driver's seat, we humans cannot do many things that need doing. But as long as the will acts as the engine, all of the rest of the cars in the train follow. Feelings come along, too. Whereas we didn't feel like praying at the start, if we remember whom we serve and exercise the will to reach out to God, we gain the added benefit of feeling glad, afterwards, that we have prayed. The feelings follow the will. We often want to continue in His presence; and all weariness has fled.

Willingness to pray with another is something that grows by degrees. "It started with a simple mealtime grace, asking God's blessing on our food," say Roger and Kathryn Railey of their now-vibrant prayer life together. "We both vocalized this together. Later on we started adding more petitions. It evolved slowly; it was not something we just jumped into."

Saying "the blessing" is about all most folks want at the start of a meal. We all are eager to begin eating. But many couples have found that while they are at the table, after the meal, is the perfect time to launch their prayer life together. Remember, we are only recommending two minutes at the start; it should almost always be possible to linger that long!

An experience of spiritual renewal can work wonders with willingness, as Betty and Gene Addison discovered. "We began to make prayer together a daily part of our lives about eleven years after we were married," says Betty, "when we heard a couple share how they prayed for each other out loud each morning, and how much it had strengthened their marriage. From that time Gene and I began to make our prayers for each other a daily practice and have continued it for twenty-two years."

A similar story is told by my sister, Nancy Mapes, and her husband, Bob, of Corpus Christi, Texas: "Prayer together for us took on greater importance after we had a deep personal renewal and experienced a growth spurt spiritually. We started fasting and praying one morning a week with our five children when they were still at home and continued setting aside prayer time as a couple after they were grown."

Marriage Encounter weekends have been used of God to launch a number of couples into regular prayer together. Joe and Mary Anne Kolten of Doylestown, Pennsylvania, attended such a weekend and returned home with a commitment to the M.E. discipline of daily dialogue. A part of this dialogue includes writing a letter to the other partner each day. "We started praying before reading each other's love letters," recalls Mary Anne. "One of the many aspects of the conversion that took place through Marriage Encounter was that we did not ever want to take our prayer life and spirituality for granted again. Couple prayer was a natural outgrowth of our desire for couple unity."

Another couple, Robert and Jackie Rickover of Marietta, Georgia, trace the beginning of their prayer life together to before they were married. "Our first experiences of praying as a couple began while we were dating and continued as newlyweds." Even with this foundation, however, willingness remained a hurdle. "Informal prayer at home was difficult for us together and continues to be after twenty-six years!" Other couples also have confessed that even after many years praying with someone else can be challenging. They would agree with Jackie Rickover who adds, "Right now, after a quarter-century of marriage, after praying together on our knees in our home, by a child's hospital bed, my mother's deathbed, our son's jail cell . . . we still are shy. Experience does not seem to erase the basic personality traits that we have to deal with constantly in order to share our faith life."

Obstacles to prayer must be "dealt with constantly" in every marriage—because the pluses of daily prayer together so far outweigh the hindrances. Kell and Ann, whose prayer commitment we described in chapter 2, are still going strong with their daily devotional time after 37 years.

"From the beginning of our marriage," Ann writes, "we've set aside an after-breakfast time of Bible reading and prayer, as well as a pre-bedtime prayer as we sought to make Christ the center of our home." That high and worthy goal, "to make Christ the center," I suspect is the key factor that has kept Kell and Ann motivated through the years.

To place Christ at the center of our homes means, of course, to tell Him, "You are our God," not just at prayer time but all day long. I cannot be careless or insensitive in what I say to Pam and then pray with her. Nor can either of us treat anyone else rudely or engage in gossip and criticism, or allow conceit and pride to rule our relations with others, and expect God to hear our prayers at the end of the day.

Praying together involves the family finances, how we spend our time, what we do for entertainment, the thoughts we dwell upon when we are apart. I cannot be dishonest or profligate or stingy in money matters and then pray with my wife for His blessing on our economic life. Nor can we be cavalier with the way we spend money on clothes or a vacation or a new car, and then pray for the poor. I cannot harbor jealousy or hatred or lust or self-conceit in my thoughts, nor can Pam, and then expect God to hear us as we pray. When we come into His presence God searches our hearts. "Surely you desire truth in the inner parts" (Psalm 51:6).

Of course we fail in many of these areas, many times. Are we hypocrites, then, when we presume to pray, knowing how unworthy we are? No, because God *loves* us. If we are aware of wrongdoing in the day just past, and acknowledge this before Him as we come together to pray, we can know that He forgives and "inclines His ear" to hear whatever we go on to ask. What we are saying here is that praying together requires that we be ourselves before God. In a church in the Midwest some years ago I heard this introduction to a study on prayer: "The first prayer should be this: May it be the *true God* to whom I am praying, and may it be the *true me* who is approaching Him." The "true me" must not think he or she is putting anything past God.

Praying with another person makes a further demand. In prayer with another I must allow that person to be himself or herself too. This is why earlier we said that prayer together is the doorway to intimacy. Ask yourself, If my marriage partner is not willing to pray with me, am I at fault? Am I forbearing and forgiving? Have I allowed the ninefold fruit of the Spirit to come forth in my life—as love, joy, peace, patience, kindness, goodness, faithfulness, gentleness and self-control (Galatians 5:22–23)? Praying together as husband and wife does not demand that the two of us have "arrived" at all these virtues, just that we confess our need of them in overcoming the other's resistance to the vulnerability prayer requires.

Being willing for prayer together is a big hurdle. But we believe that every Christian couple can clear that hurdle and go on to run the race until Christ comes or death separates one from the other.

To give you a place where you can drive down a stake and declare, "We will be prayer partners," a statement of commitment is provided here. Each partner is to sign it when both are ready. You may want to copy the page and place your signed statement in some conspicuous spot in your home for as long as you need to be reminded of your covenant and united desire for a life of prayer as husband and wife.

Our Commitment to Pray Together

On this day _____ we, _____
and _____ , covenant together with God's help
to seek the Lord in prayer together each day, for His
blessing on our marriage and for His mercy in this
world. To God be the glory. Amen.

"If two of you agree on earth about anything that they
may ask, it shall be done for them by My Father who is
in heaven" (Matthew 18:19, NASB).

Now we are ready to mark out the practical steps in
establishing a life of prayer together.

6

A Time and Place to Pray

But I call to God, and the Lord saves me.
Evening, morning and noon I cry out in distress,
  and he hears my voice.   **Psalm 55:16–17**

Daniel . . . went home to his upstairs room where the
windows opened toward Jerusalem. Three times a
day he got down on his knees and prayed, giving
thanks to his God, just as he had done before.
                                    Daniel 6:10

He writes . . .

Today we are on Mustang Island, at the Texas shore,
where, beyond the grassy sand dunes and picture-perfect
beach, the emerald waters of the Gulf of Mexico stretch to
the south and east. It is all I can do to stay at the writing
this morning, for having grown up far inland in Dallas,
whenever I am near an ocean beach the magnet-like power
of the ceaseless waves draws me shoreward.

This morning I have already once followed my heart
and gone for a walk along the pristine shore, stopping now
and then to look out toward the shimmering waters or
examine a common shell that yet looks uncommonly beautiful to my eyes. I have thought how the sea is doing here
today what I have ever seen it doing at California's south-

ern beaches and on the Jersey shore and at Hastings in southern England, where Pam grew up. From some unknown point out in the ocean the sea appears to be moving toward the shore, and then back, in ceaseless motion, but always maintaining a constant presence with the shoreline. Again this morning I could see the traces of the latest high tide, reminding me that twice within every 24 hours the ocean reaches out and up as far as it can and kisses the shore.

This rhythm of nature reassures me that some things do not change in our world. But thinking as I am today of time and place, I am intrigued with the role of these elements in the sea's existence. Regularly, year in, year out, it keeps its twice-a-day appointment with the shore, all along earth's thousands of miles of varied coastline, advancing and receding. I know that it is obeying the decree of its Maker, and that it can do no other, although I do not know how nature works this regular rhythm of the tides.

Man and sea alike live out their existence within the constant framework of day and night, day and night. Men and women are called to walk with God, as the sea is called to walk with the shore. And just as the sea twice a day hugs closer still to the shore, isn't it right for us to hug the Father and linger very near Him for a while each day? Some couples have told us that they find they want a two-a-day hug—morning and evening prayers together—and in so doing they are emulating nature's primal rhythm.

Charles Spurgeon, taking his cue from the Psalm text at the head of this chapter, makes a strong case for three hugs a day, morning, noon and night. "The three periods chosen are most fitting," he says. "To begin, continue, and end the day with God is supreme wisdom. Where time has naturally set up a boundary, there let us set up an altar-stone. The psalmist means that he will always pray; he will run a line of prayer right along the day, and track the sun with his petitions."

You have chosen to "hug" the Father together with your mate every day in a time of prayer. Especially if you are just beginning a prayer discipline as wife and husband, you will want to be as regular as the tides in keeping your "hug times."

What time of day will you pray together? And where?

Setting the Time

In choosing the time for your daily prayer together, begin by asking yourselves at what times of the day you are already with each other. This is most important on work days; presumably you have more control over the use of time on your "off" days.

You may find that the only times you two are normally together are breakfast, supper and when sleeping. In a simpler era when most families lived on farms, a couple could expect to be together as regular as clockwork for three meals and all of a long evening. Today, with both partners often working away from the home, perhaps on differing shifts, and with a variety of outside commitments, you may find you see each other only after nine P.M., and (perhaps) at breakfast. (We two believe in breakfast, and couldn't function without it!)

A second question to ask is: When are we both together *and awake?* More than one couple with whom we have talked have raised this rather obvious point. Praying together consistently requires that neither party be too wiped out for prayer. Waldron and Sharon Teague of Dallas, a couple with children, told us, "We *make* time, we don't *find* time. Sometimes it may be in the morning, but for us it is more often at night. The best time is 'prime time' before both of us are too sleepy to be at our best."

Other couples echo Sharon's point about making time. The McCaskills, who have prayed daily together 37 years, say emphatically, "We pray twice a day—after breakfast and before bedtime—and make it a priority to be at home together at both of those hours." When their three sons were growing up, all the family joined in prayer at the breakfast table; they prayed as a couple, for things of more concern just to the two of them, at bedtime.

Jeanette and David Bassett of Grand Prairie, Texas, have not let the fact that one is a night owl and the other a morning person deprive them of praying together. Jeanette says her "peak hours" are midnight to two A.M., while David's are five to six A.M. They have chosen the late evening for prayer together. "This time of day," Jeanette adds, "is freer of occupational and family responsibilities than earlier in the evening."

Dick and Carole Summers of Rockport, Texas, another morning person/night person duo, also pray in the evening. Carole, the night person, says that after their prayer time she reads while Dick goes to sleep. Richard Allen, an American missionary to Spain, acknowledges he is a night owl while his wife, Valerie, is a morning person. "This kept us from praying together for some time. We found that we desperately needed to pray and seek the Lord together so we agreed on a common time in the early evening—a time that would be good for both of us."

Breakfast time and right after supper appear to be the most popular times, though almost as many couples named bedtime as their preference. Quite a few told us they have their prayer time before getting out of bed in the morning.

"It's a wonderful way to begin a day," says Betsy Chapple of California.

As for Pam and me, we both actually prefer the morning. In Waco when I was the only one leaving home in the morning for work, we took our prayer notebook to the breakfast table and prayed following the meal. That hour has a lot going for it. Such godly persons as Moses, David and Daniel set the example of morning prayers. Of Jesus also it was said that He went apart to pray early in the morning. And praying in the morning takes literally Jesus' instruction to "seek first the kingdom of heaven" (Matthew 6:33). In practical terms, however, Pam and I are committed to individual devotions first thing in the morning. In Waco we got up at six o'clock and went apart for prayer. Then at seven, after I had dressed for work, we ate and committed ourselves and our joint prayer concerns for the day to God. It took me only eight or ten minutes to get to the office, so we could count on twenty minutes or so for prayer. It *is* a wonderful way to begin the day!

After moving to Dallas, where Pam took an outside job too, we continued to pray in the morning—or at least we tried. The habit was established and we weren't anticipating difficulties. But we were now rising at 5:30 and I was leaving for my commute to the office at 7:05, which led us soon to admit there simply was not adequate time in the morning—unless we pushed our rising hour back to five o'clock, which seemed extreme.

Thus we sought another time and it was not hard to discover. The first half hour after the evening meal would be our "prime time."

Although appointments in connection with our work at the university sometimes keep us busy in the evenings, when we are home we strive to keep our habits simple and domestic. We don't go out shopping or attend any regular event during the work week and we have only one favorite television show—a Friday night half-hour program that we always hope will live up to its billing as comedy. Thanks to the videocassette recorder, we can postpone watching the evening news until a time convenient for us. A telephone answering machine takes early evening calls. We have agreed that the ironing and reading and bill-paying and telephoning can wait till after our prayer season. So, without much ado, Pam and I turn toward prayer after the meal. I wouldn't say we rush our meals in order to pray, but we don't linger at the table either. If my son Jim is living at home, as he is now, he understands that we will want to be undisturbed while we are praying together and he usually handles the kitchen clean-up.

As I emphasized earlier, when a couple is starting out to pray together daily they need to be as regular as the incoming tides, and not allow exceptions to interfere with the appointed time. Remember, for beginners we are recommending a minimum of only two minutes each day. Five minutes will seem like an hour to the inexperienced, and so the essential thing here is to keep the prayer time every day as a concentrated and undistracted time and to increase its duration only as is mutually agreed upon.

No one can tell you how much time you should eventually give to daily prayer. One couple remarked that they pray even about that, and are asking God to make it possible for them to spend more time in prayer together. In a sense, one could never get finished praying. We might take the command to pray "without ceasing" and for "all people" so literally that we would start praying through the city phone book, and then go to the library and pray through all of the phone books there. We don't think God has called us to that.

Paul outdid us all when it comes to praying. He said once that he was praying for certain people because "I have you in my heart" (Philippians 1:7). Let this be your guide. Seek to remember those who are on your hearts, and to be faithful in praying for them by name and in specific ways.

The connection between the time of day you pray and the time given to prayer is not unimportant. For maturing Christians, sufficient time will be needed to lift to God the thanksgivings and petitions and intercessions He is impressing on you. The hour selected should be chosen in part because the couple knows that enough time will then be available to cover the prayer territory God seems to be assigning to them.

Agreeing on the Place

As Pam and I write this, we are not sure what importance God puts on the place where you pray. We are agreed that most important of all is that we actually pray. Next comes the selection of a time. Place will follow.

It used to be exactly the opposite. *Place* was important, and *time* was secondary. After God appeared to Moses on Mount Sinai, until the death of Christ, the believer oriented his or her life around the place that God had chosen on earth as His dwelling place, His Tabernacle. The Lord "met" Israel at the mercy seat, over the Ark of the Covenant, between the two cherubim. When Solomon erected the Temple to replace the temporary Tabernacle, God met His chosen people in this most holy place. In the Bible passage quoted at the beginning of this chapter the exiled

Daniel prayed at a window facing toward Jerusalem, the site of the Temple, the place God had chosen—for that time—as His earthly point of rendezvous with man.

But all of that changed with the coming of Christ. We look back now and realize that time and place converged once and for all on a hill outside Jerusalem where Jesus Christ became sin for us. From that time on, the veil has been torn from the most holy place and the way has been made for God to dwell in every human heart: "I am with you until the end of the age" (Matthew 28:20).

So today, we believers can meet God anyplace.

Does place have any importance, then? We believe that it has. Just as having an appointed time and place lets us keep an appointment with another person, having a place to go for prayer together is just one small step further toward making this a habit. A variety of places has been mentioned as "first choices"—in bed, at the kitchen table, in the living room, on the front porch swing, while walking, while driving, or, as one couple said, "wherever our two-year-old has something to do." Some couples have told us that "wherever there's privacy" is a place where they can pray.

Others pray always in the same place. One couple, lay leaders in their church, call the living room sofa their "sanctuary" and make it a habit to meet God there. Another couple pray on the couch in the family room: "It's a comfortable place, with a huge picture of Jesus facing us over the fireplace mantle."

Chuck and Pat Bianco also prefer the living room sofa for their daily prayer time. "When the kids were very young," Chuck recalls, "we just prayed louder than they talked!" Chuck underlines the value of a couple's not retiring to a bedroom for prayer: "If the children do not see us praying together, how will they learn to pray?"

Husbands and wives who have their prayer time at the same place day by day could point to the Lord Jesus as their example, for we read that Jesus had a habit of going to the Mount of Olives for prayer (Luke 22:39).

Our usual habit is to pray at the table after the dishes have been removed, for there we can sit side by side and open the prayer notebook on the table. At present, however, Jim is usually at home during our prayer time. Because of the way our home is designed, to remain at the table for prayer would block him off from the whole rear part of the house, so we may beat a retreat upstairs to our bedroom to pray, or retire to the navy blue armchairs in the front room.

In talking with others we were glad to learn that many people get on their knees for their prayer time. That is an infrequent posture for us—we usually pray sitting—but when either the blessings of God or the needs of the moment have brought a special sense of His awesomeness, we do pray from a kneeling position. Some people, however, cannot long remain on their knees with comfort. Better to pray from a comfortable position, with the mind fixed on God, than on one's knees with the mind fixed on how uncomfortable one is! It is possible for the body to be comfortably resting in a chair while the heart is on its knees.

In summary, it *is* important for a couple to set a time for "hugging" the Father each day. We have not discussed the weekends. For ourselves, on Saturdays we try to come aside for prayer following breakfast. Structure-less Saturday can be either a godsend or a disaster. We find that taking time to pray in the morning is an excellent insurance against losing our focus on Him in a whirl of activity. On Sunday, with its times of corporate worship, we do not try to schedule prayer together.

It is important also to have a location for daily prayer. In fact, judging from our experience, having two or three places is good, if possible, so that you have an alternate if your chosen spot is not available.

The important thing, though, is to pray as a couple—whenever, wherever—daily, twice, thrice a day. Pray! Pray! Pray!

7

Structure for Daily Prayer Together

I urge, then, first of all, that requests, prayers, intercession and thanksgiving be made for *everyone*—for
kings and all those in authority, that we may live
peaceful and quiet lives in all godliness and holiness.
1 Timothy 2:1–2

She writes . . .

That challenging word *everyone* in Paul's letter to Timothy reminds us that a certain amount of disciplined structure is necessary if Carey and I are to be serious
intercessors. How can we possibly hope to pray for everybody? Obviously two people cannot and are not meant to,
but two people can seek to be obedient and pray for those
whom we are "given." And we can encourage others to
pray also so that the worldwide Christian Church together
fulfills the command and "everybody" is prayed for.

In our separate daily quiet times immediately after rising each day, Carey and I use an identical set of Bible
study notes. (They happen to be *Daily Notes* published by
Scripture Union in England.) Dated study aids help us be
disciplined in reading the Scriptures.

And the discipline of structure helps us in prayer as

well. This is not to suggest that prayer can ever be reduced to a formula. A study of the prayers of the Bible shows us that every petition recorded in Scripture is different. There is no "method" to the prayers in the Bible. God looks at the heart, not the technique.

Still, experienced pray-ers take care to include the various aspects of this ministry. Gene and Betty Addison write: "The elements of our prayers together consist of praising the Lord, giving thanks to Him and intercession for others. Then we close with our statement/creed which is

>Jesus is Lord,
>Jesus is my Lord,
>Jesus is our Lord.

"We find this affirmation an excellent way of stating our belief together before the Lord."

When Carey and I allow our prayer time to be entirely spontaneous, we find that selfishness soon takes over. We will seek the Father's help and blessing but we may fail to approach Him with the worship, humility and gratitude due the King of kings. Some such framework as the acronym ACTS, therefore, mentioned earlier, can be of great help in keeping before us four ingredients of true prayer:

Adoration
Confession
Thanksgiving
Supplication

(Somebody said to me recently, "I often think the acronym should be CATS since before I can adore the Father, I need frequently to confess my sin to Him.")

Adoration. In our prayer times I often wait for Carey to pray first because he puts words of praise to God together in ways in which I am not yet able, weaving words of Scripture into his own offering. Here is how Carey expressed joy and praise one day for answered prayer following years of waiting:

"What can I render unto You, O Lord, for Your exceeding great kindness to me? How shall I tell of all Your gentle nurture and unfailing encouragement? I am without words to tell how glad and overjoyed I am. O that I could enter into Your presence and cast myself at Your feet to say, 'Our God reigns! He lives! He hears the prayers of His people and takes pity on them!' Praise You, Lord. When I had almost fainted, I believed to see Your goodness in the land of the living. When I almost despaired, I heard You saying, Hope in God—for you shall yet praise Him! Bless the Lord, O my soul. And all that is within me, bless His holy name."

I believe God is pleased with that kind of eloquent, elegantly worded praise. I tend to follow a beaten path in my expressions of adoration and have to admit I often find them boring even to myself! God is gracious and He will accept my prayer, but I believe I need to work at being less repetitive.

In our times of adoration, Carey and I are helped when we meditate on the greatness and attributes of God before trying to put our adoration into words. We try to come into His presence quietly and reverently together. If we have started with Scripture reading, one of us may offer praise and thanksgiving for something the Bible text contained. If we have sung a hymn we may repeat words of praise to the Lord from that source.

Confession. This is usually the shortest section of our prayer time, and the same is true of most of the praying couples whom we have interviewed. All too often confession turns quickly into supplication. I might pray: "Lord, before I can present requests to You tonight with my husband, I need to confess a complaining spirit today about this endless Texas heat. It wears me out. Will there never come an end to summer? Please help me bear it." My prayer of confession ended at the close of the first sentence!

I notice in my prayer time with Carey, and in prayer with other Christians, that few of us know simply how to confess sin, claim the forgiveness of the Lord and put the sin behind us. To pray, "Forgive us our sins"—though it is a good start—is not confession and will not serve to put any sin behind us. When we do confess specifics, however, the problem area all too often dominates and then overrides the element of confession. In chapter 8 we will give some examples of prayers of real confession made by others that have been of great help to us.

Thanksgiving. This should be one of the easiest parts of prayer, the recounting of answers to prayers and blessings received. But we are forgetful people. Because we are forgetful, we find the recording of prayer requests in a notebook, with dates, and space for follow-up insights and answers, of great value in building the habit of gratitude. Carey and I try to recall as many reasons within the past 24 hours as we can for which to thank the Lord before entering the fourth stage of prayer.

Supplication. This is bringing our requests to God. It can be further divided into *intercession,* which is supplication for others, and *petition,* which is supplication on our own behalf.

Different Types of Supplication

First are our *specific* requests, the kind of prayer that lays hold of God with urgency. It is definite by nature. We use this kind of prayer when beseeching the Lord to intervene in the lives of family members and friends. I believe God likes it when we are definite in what we ask. Yet it is much easier to be vague. Vague prayer does not require much faith either in the making or in the waiting for the answer.

Brother Andrew is a man of definite prayer. His book *God's Smuggler* recounts God's definite answers to such supplication. An example is "the smuggler's prayer" that Brother Andrew taught his teams to pray as they took Bibles behind the Iron Curtain. I went on a number of these trips between 1968 and 1976 and I prayed "the smuggler's prayer" from my heart just before approaching the border of various Communist lands:

> Lord Jesus, when You were on earth You sometimes made blind eyes to see. Today we ask You to do the opposite. You know that in our cars we have Bibles and help for the Christians to whom Your Word is denied. Will You please make the seeing eyes of the border guards blind for just an instant so they will not see what we have with us?

Again and again we saw God answer that definite prayer.

A joyful recent instance is the conversion of my brother, "Digger" Rosewell. Carey and I prayed, "Lord, show Digger his need of You." When my brother came to the point of making Jesus Christ Lord of his life, he explained in a transAtlantic call, "For the first time I saw my need of Him"—using the very phrase we had prayed! Another specific prayer of ours and of thousands worldwide was that God would remove from authority the Romanian dictator Ceaucescu. It seemed impossible; the despot's cruel grip on the people was vise-like. Yet I can hear as if it happened yesterday my husband's voice that Christmas of 1989 when he called from his office to tell me, "Ceaucescu has fled the palace in Bucharest."

But there are times when we cannot be specific. Sometimes we do not know how to suggest that God should intervene in a situation. There is an example of what I call nonspecific prayer in John 2. The Lord Jesus and His disciples are at a wedding feast in Cana where the wine has run out. The mother of Jesus comes to Him and says, "They have no more wine." She simply states the problem. She does not tell the Lord Jesus what she thinks He should do about it, but leaves the matter with Him. She knows He has a solution to the situation she has described. The Lord answered her prayer, nonspecific as it was, and provided the best wine at the marriage feast.

Carey and I sometimes do not know how to pray about a particular need. At those times we simply state the problem to the Lord. We do not ask Him to do anything specific because we do not know what is best, but we know that He does have the right solution and the very best timing for the answer. "In the same way, the Spirit helps us in our weakness. We do not know what we ought to pray for, but the Spirit himself intercedes for us with groans that words cannot express" (Romans 8:26).

Nonspecific prayer can be every bit as heartfelt and passionate as specific prayer. It can be the kind that Jehoshaphat, king of Judah, prayed. We find the story in 2 Chronicles 20. Facing the combined armies of Moab and Ammon, the king cries out to the Lord, "We have no power to face this vast army that is attacking us. *We do not know what to do, but our eyes are upon you*" (verse 12).

I remember clearly praying Jehoshaphat's prayer one desperate June day in 1982. At the start of Corrie's illness

I had promised her that I would be with her until "the glorious new beginning," as she referred to her death. When she became severely incapacitated, I decided I would not leave her for periods longer than part of a day. This decision met a severe test when I learned that my mother was diagnosed with a malignancy. I longed to travel to England to be with my mother, to whom I was particularly close. She made my dilemma much easier by insisting I stay with Tante Corrie, but the anguish of my heart is still reflected in the margin of my Bible. Next to Jehoshaphat's words, I penciled in the date in June when my heart cried out, "Lord, I do not know what to do, but my eyes are upon You." I simply told the Lord that I did not know how to handle this situation and left it with Him.

Ten months later, the Lord took Tante Corrie to heaven and then gave me the privilege of being with my mother until her own homegoing later the same year. Although these two vigils following one another so swiftly were agonizingly hard, the Lord honored my desperate nonspecific prayer and allowed me to care for both Tante Corrie and my mother at the end of their lives.

Another kind of supplication is fervent, tenacious, long-term intercession on behalf of others. This is the sort of prayer that does not give up, even if the answer is years in coming. It is prayer that echoes Jacob's cry to God in Genesis 32:26, "I will not let you go unless you bless me." It is the kind of prayer one couple we know are praying for their two beloved daughters, 18 and 22, who are not in touch with them. Their continued absence forces the parents again and again, many times a day, to cry out to the Father, "Lord, work out Your perfect will in their lives. Give them hearts that want to do Your will. Prosper them, keep them healthy, surround them with good influences."

However long answers are in coming, this mother and father will not cease storming heaven for their children.

These, then, are various emphases in supplication, with the ACTS structure standing like invisible scaffolding behind our daily prayer practice.

The Prayer Notebook

Each evening after supper when the dishes have been cleared from the table, Carey goes to our bedroom and takes from a drawer of his bedside table our white three-ring binder prayer book. The fact that he keeps it there among his most personal possessions is an indication to me of the importance of this book in his life. He never puts it on a bookshelf, for this is not just any book. It contains our prayer list, a record of our talks with God as husband and wife. In the notebook we record requests and dates, updating entries as situations change. When a prayer is answered, that is recorded too, with the date.

Before we met, Carey and I had established the habit individually of praying for "causes"—often mission organizations and government authorities—as well as family and friends. While we were becoming adjusted to the happy state of matrimony we prayed awhile without the aid of a list of any kind. But this meant neglecting certain needs and we both soon felt constrained to a more disciplined effort. This led us to draw up a list of our combined prayer concerns, but it also brought a dilemma. How would we pray for all these people? We knew we could not intercede for all of them every day.

Carey came up with the solution of dividing our prayer list into six parts, one for each day of the week, designating an "area" of concern to each day. As we said earlier, we knew that we could not pray for the whole world, nor did we think God expected that of us. What we have been led to is the "adoption" of certain people and geopolitical areas of the world; there we will concentrate our prayers on a sustained basis.

Our particular structure for daily supplication is this:

Monday—pray for our nations' leaders, local and state or county authorities

Tuesday—pray for light in a spiritually dark land (we remember those in the spiritual darkness of Islam)

Wednesday—intercede for specific missionaries

Thursday—pray for the suffering Church (we pray for Eastern Europe and the former Soviet Union)

Friday—intercede for family and friends

Saturday—pray for the Jews, for urban missions and our local church

Here is a more specific listing.

Monday. We pray for those in authority in the United States and in England, naming the President and the Prime Minister and members of their cabinets. We intercede for them in current world or national crises. We ask God to help them humble themselves before Him and seek His guidance. Based on Daniel's prayer below, Carey and I call out to God for His mercy on our countries. We remind Him of that which He already knows, that we are a disobedient, violent people who have not sought Him as we should, asking His forgiveness for sins of commission and omission. We pray the same for our metropolitan area, trying to ask in the spirit of Daniel:

> "Now, our God, hear the prayers and petitions of your servant. For your sake, O Lord, look with favor

on your desolate sanctuary. Give ear, O God, and hear; open your eyes and see the desolation of the city that bears your Name. We do not make requests of you because we are righteous, but because of your great mercy. O Lord, listen! O Lord, forgive! O Lord, hear and act! For your sake, O my God, do not delay."

Daniel 9:17–19

Material provided by the Dallas Prayer Ministry for the yearly national day of prayer gives us the names of national and local political leaders. Intercessors for America (P.O. Box 2639, Reston, VA 22090) also gives useful information for the kind of prayer we make on Monday night.

Tuesday. "Prayer unlocks the world's most difficult doors," a quote used by Open Doors with Brother Andrew, is one we keep before us on Tuesday evening. Every Tuesday we devote a portion of our prayer time to that part of the world under Muslim domination.

In our Tuesday evening section of the three-ring binder we are gathering information about the Islamic lands and filing prayer letters and photographs of missionaries both known and unknown to us. This section also contains a world map giving the distribution of Muslims and we try to name as many of the countries as possible before the Lord.

Tuesday night prayer is perhaps the most difficult of the entire week. We were praying for the Muslim world on another night of the week, but because that night was constantly interrupted by other engagements, we switched to Tuesday. On "Muslim night" we can still count on all sorts of things trying to interfere, but we recognize that such static often comes from Satan. The devil has held millions of people in bondage for fourteen hundred years, but today light is breaking through. On this evening we often claim the promise in Psalm 2: "Lord, you have said, 'Ask of me, and I will make the nations your inheritance, and the ends of the earth your possession' (verse 8). Lord, make these nations Your nations!" We also sometimes recite aloud the prayer for Muslim lands found in chapter 8.

Wednesday. On this evening we pray for specific missionaries and for Vimala, in India, our sponsored child. This section of our prayer book contains photographs and prayer letters to refresh our memories about their situations. Other couples use mission materials the same way.

George Cowan, former president of Wycliffe Bible Translators, told us, "My wife, Florrie, and I keep a folder of all mission bulletins, etc., to pray through following breakfast. When we're able to be together at lunchtime, we pray for a particular country of the world, going through the book *Operation World* page by page and recalling 1 Timothy 2:1–2: 'I urge, then, first of all, that requests, prayers, intercession and thanksgiving be made for everyone—for kings and all those in authority.'"

Ruth and Mac Aipperspach, college faculty in Corpus Christi, Texas, say, "At suppertime after devotions we use the Southern Baptist Foreign Mission Prayer Update and several other monthly publications, such as the Bible Society calendar, on a rotating basis. We usually take three requests an evening."

Thursday. On this evening we pray for Eastern Europe, including the former Soviet Union. We continually thank God for the miracle of the collapse of Communism and the measure of freedom that has come to the Church in this region. Carey and I have both worked and traveled on behalf of the Church in Eastern Europe, and we pray for Christians there by name, bringing before the Lord their requests as we receive them. We also pray for their governments and church leaders.

Friday. Our prayer time on this evening is devoted to our family and friends and any of their individual needs known to us.

Saturday. On this day, the Jewish sabbath, seeking to obey the Lord's command in Psalm 122:6, we pray for the peace of Jerusalem and for the salvation of the Jews. We ask the Lord that peace may come to Israel by their coming to know the Prince of Peace. Our prayers are assisted by newsletters from Jewish missions, including Jews for Jesus. On this day we also intercede for our own church and for Christian ministries in the world's urban centers.

We also have a personal page or two in our binder where we list our own requests and those for our family, my speaking appointments, etc. Here is a sample from this section of our notebook—extremely simple, but an enormous help to us in our desire to be consistent intercessors. (The names have been changed.)

Charlene & Doug—healing for C 7–12–91
Neil, Anne, Kathy—Lord's leading where & when
Jeff—God's leading for job; 7–22–91—his hearing in
*   hospital, help for his mental state 10–91—good work &*
*   independence*
Beverly & Gill 6–6–91—marriage in trouble; Bev to see
*   reason to stay*
Tom & Jean Olson—praise God for work provided;
*   3–15–91—sale of house & his leading in May*

As Carey has mentioned, we don't schedule a prayer time on Sundays, although we do feel it necessary at some point on many Sundays to lay before God our needs and especially the challenges of the upcoming week.

Carey and I believe that the Lord is not looking for extraordinary men or women with special gifts of intercession. He is simply looking for obedient men and women. We want to be found faithful by the Lord. We are not special or unusual, but He will take even us, and the simple acronym and the helpful tool of our prayer book. He can use us and every ordinary Christian couple to "stand in the gap" in a dark time in the history of the world.

8

"Take with You Words": Models for Our Prayer Life

"Take with you words, and return to the Lord."
Hosea 14:2, RSV

She writes . . .

In this chapter, to which we have very much looked forward, Carey and I want to share some favorite prayers that have given wings to our prayer life. But please don't misunderstand what is intended here. Couples don't *need* finely worded prayers to reach God. He has never placed a requirement on the *wording* of our prayers—only on our hearts' condition, and that we come in Jesus' name. He hears the most untaught tongue that truly calls on Him.

And conversely, "saying a prayer" that is eloquent and beautiful does *not* guarantee that the prayer is heard. In a sense this is the most unneeded chapter in the book, for you can come to God and say what you mean with reverence and trust, and even if you get the words mixed up God will hear and will answer.

Those who grew up with written prayers, in fact, may need to develop spontaneity and learn to use composed prayers less frequently. But many of us did not grow up in this way, and for us this chapter is important indeed. At the outset we may hesitate, not knowing if one can truly pray from someone else's words. All Carey and I can say is, try—and proof will follow.

There are times when every couple needs to know how to pray. Then the hundreds of prayers in the Bible can guide us. The prayers of the Church, which have withstood the test of time, can also help us pray aright. James says, for example, that we need help in our praying so that we will not be selfish (James 4:2–3).

Many prayers have been set to music and are found in our hymnals and songbooks. They can serve a double purpose for husbands and wives, causing us to sing together, which for many is a delight. And the words of the best hymns lead us to pray beyond our knowledge and experience, to pray with words inspired by the angels and wrung from the discipline of saintly souls.

It is not a common practice these days for husbands and wives to write out their prayers, but our research shows that Christians in previous centuries did so, leaving us with telling and immensely helpful records. In offering magnificent prayers that Christians through the centuries have prayed, we ascend in worship to the very throne of God. We sense the reality of the "cloud of witnesses" with which we are surrounded and know that we are joining in the prayers of the Church triumphant. Thus lifted up we are strengthened for daily life.

Written prayers, whether from the Word of God or from the prayer book or the hymnal or some other source, can particularly aid us when we are weak or sick or disheartened. Another advantage is that praying together need never get boring!

Hosea the prophet longed for Israel to mend her ways. Note what he did not do, and what he did. Hosea did not counsel more sacrifices and offerings. No, he instructed

Israel "take with you words and return to the Lord." All that Israel, the people of God, had to do was to open their mouths and offer words of confession, of thanksgiving and of recommittal.

In the pages that follow are words for you. Take them, learn some by heart, pray them aloud to God with your marriage partner. And see if God does not meet you there.

The prayer best known to most Christians is the Lord's Prayer. In answer to the disciples' plea "Teach us to pray!" the Lord Jesus gave us this model, incorporating praise, submission to God's will, confession, forgiveness of others, and supplication both for daily necessities and protection from Satan:

> "Our Father in heaven,
> hallowed be your name,
> your kingdom come,
> your will be done
>   on earth as it is in heaven.
> Give us today our daily bread.
> Forgive us our debts,
>   as we also have forgiven our debtors.
> And lead us not into temptation,
> but deliver us from the evil one,
> for yours is the kingdom and the power and the glory
> forever. Amen."   Matthew 6:9–13

To pray the Lord's Prayer involves much more than reciting the words of the Lord Jesus. To the disciples' request the Lord answered, "Pray like this," meaning, "Align your heart and will with these words and you will come to understand how to pray." (One of the most helpful explanations of the Lord's Prayer we have read recently is in chapter 8 of Brother Andrew's book *And God Changed His Mind.*)

We have organized the prayers that follow in subject areas, again using the acronym ACTS. As you repeat portions of these words, let the Spirit prime your own pump and call you to prayer as He leads.

Adoration

Many instances of praise and adoration in the Bible are "user-friendly" for partners in prayer. Some of our favorites are these, which can serve well to launch a prayer session, verbalized either by one partner or both.

Come, let us worship and bow down;
Let us kneel before the Lord our Maker.
For He is our God,
And we are the people of His pasture,
    and the sheep of His hand.   Psalm 95:6–7, NASB

Bless the Lord, O my soul;
And all that is within me, bless His holy name.
Bless the Lord, O my soul,
And forget none of His benefits;
Who pardons all your iniquities;
Who heals all your diseases;
Who redeems your life from the pit;
Who crowns you with lovingkindness and compassion;
Who satisfies your years with good things,
So that your youth is renewed like the eagle.
                    Psalm 103:1–5, NASB

"Praise be to you, O Lord,
    God of our father Israel,
    from everlasting to everlasting.
Yours, O Lord, is the greatness and the power
    and the glory and the majesty and the splendor,
    for everything in heaven and earth is yours.

Yours, O Lord, is the kingdom;
   you are exalted as head over all.
Wealth and honor come from you;
   you are the ruler of all things.
In your hands are strength and power
   to exalt and give strength to all.
Now, our God, we give you thanks,
   and praise your glorious name."

                       1 Chronicles 29:10–13

"You are worthy, our Lord and God,
   to receive glory and honor and power,
for you created all things,
   and by your will they were created
   and have their being."   Revelation 4:11

"Salvation belongs to our God, who sits on the throne,
and to the Lamb. . . . Praise and glory and wisdom
and thanks and honor and power and strength be to
our God forever and ever. Amen!"

                        Revelation 7:10, 12

A hymn that can either be sung or spoken aloud as an invitation to adore God is "Holy, Holy, Holy." Repetition is useful in gaining full concentration on the grandeur of the Lord.

Holy, holy, holy!
Lord God Almighty!
Early in the morning our song shall rise to Thee;
Holy, holy, holy!
Merciful and mighty!
God in three Persons, blessed Trinity!

               Reginald Heber (1783–1826)

The following hymn in its second stanza contains the only reference we know of in popular hymnody to the truth that "He gives the very best to those who leave the choice to Him":

Praise to the Lord, the Almighty, the king of creation!
O my soul praise Him, for He is thy health and salvation!
All ye who hear, Now to His temple draw near;
Join me in glad adoration!

Praise to the Lord, who o'er all things so wondrously reigneth,
Shelters thee under His wings, yes, so gently sustaineth!
Hast thou not seen how all thy longings have been
Granted in what He ordaineth?

> Joachim Neander (1650–1680)
> trans. Catherine Winkworth

Confession

As we mentioned in chapter 7, without examples to guide us, Carey and I find it difficult to concentrate on real confession. The following prayers help us.

> Almighty and most merciful Father, we have erred, and strayed from Your ways like lost sheep. We have followed too much the devices and desires of our own hearts. We have offended against Your holy laws. We have left undone those things which we ought to have done; and we have done those things which we ought not to have done; and there is no health in us. But You, O Lord, have mercy upon us, miserable offenders. Spare those, O God, who confess their faults. Restore those who are penitent, according to Your promises declared to mankind in Christ Jesus, our Lord. And grant, O most merciful Father, for His

sake, that we may hereafter live a godly and righteous
life, to the glory of Your holy name. Amen.

> Based on a General Confession from
> *The Book of Common Prayer*

David made this confession after his grievous sin, and so
can we today. (The latter part is petition, not confession,
which can also be used with much profit.)

> Have mercy on me, O God,
>   according to your unfailing love;
> according to your great compassion
>   blot out my transgressions.
> Wash away all my iniquity
>   and cleanse me from my sin.
> For I know my transgressions,
>   and my sin is always before me.
> Against you, you only, have I sinned
>   and done what is evil in your sight. . . .
> Create in me a pure heart, O God,
>   and renew a steadfast spirit within me.
> Do not cast me from your presence
>   or take your Holy Spirit from me.
> Restore to me the joy of your salvation
>   and grant me a willing spirit, to sustain me.

> Psalm 51:1–4, 10–12

> Forgive them all, O Lord:
> our sins of omission and our sins of commission;
> the sins of our youth and the sins of our riper years;
> the sins of our souls and the sins of our bodies;
> our secret and our more open sins;
> our sins of ignorance and surprise
> and our more deliberate and presumptuous sins;
> the sins we have done to please ourselves

and the sins we have done to please others;
the sins we know and remember
and the sins we have forgotten;
the sins we have striven to hide from others
and the sins by which we have made others offend;
forgive them, O Lord, forgive them all for his sake,
who died for our sins and rose for our justification,
and now stands at thy right hand to make intercession
for us, Jesus Christ our Lord.

John Wesley (1703–1791)

Thanksgiving

The following words can help us call to mind specific answers to prayer and blessings received. The Lord wants to receive our thanks. If we are forgetful we are like the nine lepers who called to the Lord for healing, received it and then went on their way without expressing gratitude. "Were not all ten cleansed? Where are the other nine?" are words from Luke 17:17 that I often hear resounding in my conscience. God uses them to remind me that at least nine times more thanks are due to Him than I am wont to give.

Give thanks to the Lord, for he is good. His love
endures forever.
Give thanks to the God of gods. His love endures
forever.
Give thanks to the Lord of lords. His love endures
forever.   Psalm 136:1–3

Thanks be to God! He gives us the victory through
our Lord Jesus Christ.   1 Corinthians 15:57

Now thank we all our God with heart and hands
     and voices,
Who wondrous things hath done, in whom His
     world rejoices;
Who, from our mother's arms, hath blest us on our
     way
With countless gifts of love, and still is ours today.

All praise and thanks to God the Father now be
     given,
The Son, and Him who reigns with them in highest
     heaven,
The one eternal God, Whom earth and heav'n
     adore;
For thus it was, is now, and shall be evermore.

Martin Rinkart (1586–1649)
trans. Catherine Winkworth

Supplication

We include here a prayer that Corrie ten Boom heard her father pray very frequently. It reminds us to hold this world and all material things lightly. It is not an escape from involvement in the world around us—Corrie's father served his neighbor at the cost of his own life—but a recognition of Christ's Lordship.

> Please, Father, let that day soon come when we will see Your beloved Son coming again in the clouds of heaven. Amen.

Casper ten Boom (1859–1944)

Here is another simple prayer that I heard Corrie ten Boom make almost daily. Life holds many perplexing difficulties for every Christian couple. How we view these difficulties affects our response to them:

Lord, help us see things from Your point of view.

For the Muslim World

Almighty God, our heavenly Father, you have made of one blood all nations, and promised that many shall come to sit down with Abraham in your kingdom. We pray for your one billion people in Muslim lands who are still far off, that they might be brought near by the blood of Christ. Look upon them in pity because they are without understanding of your truth. Take away blindness of heart, and reveal to them the surpassing beauty and power of your Son, Jesus Christ.

Convince them of their sin and pride in rejecting the sacrifice of the only Savior. Give courage to those who love you that they may boldly confess your name.

Equip your messengers in Muslim lands with the power of the Holy Spirit that they may demonstrate the loveliness and tenderness of the Lord Jesus Christ. Make bare your arm, O God, and show your power.

Father, the hour has come; glorify your Son in the Muslim world, and fulfill through him the prayer of Abraham your friend, "Oh that Ishmael might live before you." For Jesus' sake, Amen.

by Samuel Zwemer, adapted by Ronald Waine
(taken from *Ishmael My Brother**)

For Guidance

"Speak, for your servant is listening."

1 Samuel 3:10

* Co-published by World Vision International (MARC USA), Send The Light (Operation Mobilization) and the Evangelical Missionary Alliance, 1985.

For Our Children

Father, hear us, we are praying,
Hear the words our hearts are saying,
We are praying for our children.
Keep them from the power of evil,
From the secret, hidden peril,
From the whirlpool that would suck them,
From the treacherous quicksand, pluck them.
From the worldling's hollow gladness,
From the sting of faithless sadness,
Holy Father, save our children.
Through life's troubled waters steer them,
Through life's bitter battle cheer them,
Father, Father, be Thou near them.
Read the language of our longing,
Read the wordless pleadings thronging,
Holy Father, for our children.
  And wherever they may bide,
  Lead them Home at eventide.

Amy Carmichael (1867–1951)

For Love

More love to Thee, O Christ, more love to Thee!
Hear Thou the prayer I make on bended knee;
This is my earnest plea: more love, O Christ to Thee,
More love to Thee, more love to Thee!

Elizabeth P. Prentiss (1818–1878)

For the Poor

Carey's prayers are frequently for the poor and neglected. We like this prayer of Lord Shaftesbury, British reformer of the nineteenth century:

O God, the father of the forsaken, the help of the weak, the supplier of the needy; you teach us that love towards the race of man is the bond of perfectness, and the imitation of your blessed self. Open and touch our hearts that we may see and do, both for this world and that which is to come, the things that belong to our peace. Strengthen us in the work which we have undertaken; give us wisdom, perseverance, faith, and zeal, and in your own time and according to your pleasure prosper the issue; for the love of your Son Jesus Christ.

For Surrender to God's Will

"Abba, Father, everything is possible for you. Take this cup from me. Yet not what I will, but what you will."   Mark 14:36

O Lord, you know what is best for me. Let this or that be done, as you please. Give what you will, how much you will and when you will.

                                        Erasmus (1469?–1536)

Take, Lord, all my liberty,
my memory, my understanding,
and my whole will.
You have given me all that I have,
all that I am,
and I surrender all to your divine will,
that you dispose of me.
Give me only your love and your grace.
With this I am rich enough,
and I have no more to ask.

                              Ignatius Loyola (1491–1556)

Make Me Thy Fuel
From prayer that asks that I may be
Sheltered from winds that beat on Thee,
From fearing when I should aspire,
From faltering when I should climb higher,
From silken self, O Captain, free
Thy soldier who would follow Thee.

Amy Carmichael

Almighty God, who has given us grace at this time to come together to pray to You; and who promises that when two or three are gathered together in Your name You will grant their requests; fulfil now, O Lord, the desires and petitions of Your servants, as may be best for them, granting us in this world knowledge of Your truth, and in the world to come life everlasting. Amen.

Based on a prayer of St. Chrysostom in
The Book of Common Prayer

In conclusion, we are never on surer ground than when praying the very prayers found in the Bible. Look, for instance, at Colossians 1 and Ephesians 3. Paul prayed for those on his heart, and most of what he prayed can be taken up by today's intercessors. When you know what to pray, and when you do not know what to pray, these words are given to you from the Lord to give back to Him in prayer for your mate, your pastor, your friend or a missionary far away. Take with you these words and your prayer life will never be the same.

9
Warnings and Words of Caution

> And I sought for a man among them, that should
> make up the hedge, and stand in the gap before me
> for the land, that I should not destroy it: but I found
> none.   Ezekiel 22:30, KJV

He writes . . .

For you to pray together as a couple will mean so very
much to your marriage, to your family, to your church and
to your nation that we want you to be satisfied with nothing less than praying together "for as long as you both
shall live!" Thus, some warnings and cautions drawn from
the experience of couples who have been practicing daily
prayer together for years—signposts to alert you to the
potholes and detours and blind curves you may encounter
as you persist in prayer. When we know the roadblocks
along the way we can take precautions.

Beware of the Distraction of the Good

A friend said to us, "The difficult part about praying
together is keeping important things from crowding out
what is most important to our marriage—prayer!" And
Pam and I don't need to look far to realize that the *good*

does crowd out the *best*. Take last evening, for example.

We left work at the regular hour, drove home and then went to the gym for a forty-minute workout. We knew this would make supper late, but exercise, being *important*, must have its due. By seven o'clock we were home again and with Jim's help were sitting down to eat at 7:45. The three of us had plenty to talk about and the mail won its claim for attention. By this time it was nearly nine o'clock and I said, "We may as well watch the evening news," which we had videotaped earlier. Another *important* thing.

While Pam and I watched the news we enjoyed some peach cobbler, which had been baking following supper, and finally headed upstairs at 9:30. It being late, we decided to get into our night clothes and have our prayer time in bed. By ten o'clock, resting against the pillows, having talked for a while about the day's events, with our prayer book opened for the day's intercessions, we began praying. My first words were: "Father, forgive us for putting everything else before You and Your Kingdom tonight. That is sin." We both felt the lateness of the hour, and our prayers lacked earnestness and zeal, for our energies had been spent on *important* things—leaving little energy for the *most important*.

We had made a series of decisions to do other things before prayer, the best thing.

Prayer is not, of course, the only *best* thing that gets bumped by a lesser good. I remember my seminary Greek professor telling us to spread glue across the seats of our chairs whenever we started a Bible study or sermon preparation. Because prayer requires time and effort, it too calls for glue-in-the-chair stick-to-itness. Otherwise, good things—conversation, exercise, getting the car serviced, etc., etc.—will hog all the available time.

Writing is another activity that suffers from *good* distractions. Sherwood Wirt, my one-time boss, used to regale his fellow writers with his description of how a writer writes. In my own words, this is how I remember his describing a typical day.

He (or she) sits down to his typewriter—this was before the day of word processors—and rolls a clean sheet of paper into place. He stares at the page awhile. He pecks out a sentence. Again he stares at the page. Glancing up at the bookshelf he sees a row of books that needs straightening. He gets up and aligns the books, noticing in the process that one of the volumes belongs somewhere else. Extracting it from the shelf he goes to put it in its proper slot.

That done, he returns to his task and rereads what he has typed. He picks up his pencil to make a change. But his pencil has a blunt end. The pencil sharpener is in the kitchen. Now that he thinks of it, he realizes that he is thirsty. He can sharpen his pencil and get a drink at the same time. That would be wise time-budgeting.

Rising, he takes the pencil and treads downstairs to the kitchen. Going to the refrigerator he pours himself some fruit juice, watching the sparrows at the birdfeeder as he drinks. He sees that they are almost out of food, but he can't let that distract him—he is writing, he tells himself.

Returning to the stairs he notices that the blinds are closed in the living room, so he stops to open them and peers out the front to see what is going on. Happily, nothing catches his eye and he returns to his writing. He now sees a better way to begin his story and reaches for his pencil. Only his pencil is not there. He goes downstairs to get it. This time he craves a few crackers. . . .

You get the point. Writing, like prayer, suffers, not because of wicked things, but because *good things* distract and rob us of the best. This is why we must make our prayer time first priority. The answer to the problem of distractions is to go straight for prayer at the appointed time and place.

Be Ready to Put "Feet" to Your Prayers

As Pam and I write today, Tom and Lisa Ho are thirteen time zones away from their home in Plano, Texas. This couple is in Indonesia for three weeks—because of their prayers. For a year they had been praying with an increasing, consuming burden for Lisa's parents and her three sisters in that predominantly Muslim land. "Someone please tell them of God's love and of how Jesus died to save them!" they cried to God. Now Tom and Lisa have put their own feet in motion to answer their own prayers.

It is often not enough just to pray.

Prayer is the *first* thing. If all of us could learn that truth we would all know more peace and assurance in our walk with God. And prayer is the *next* thing as well. We are called to persevere in prayer. But though sometimes all we can do is pray, that is frequently not the case.

Have you found that praying about a matter is like turning on the ignition? Prayer gets not only soul and spirit but the body, too, in motion toward the desired goal. If you are praying for a sick friend you may find that your prayers lead you to that friend's bedside. If you are praying for food relief for starving populations in Ethiopia you may find yourself writing a check. If you are praying for a group of people that does not have a church or even one book of the Bible in their own language, you may find yourself volunteering to go yourself.

No doubt, this is one reason why couples do not pray together. They are afraid of the consequences! Until we have understood Calvary love all of us want to get to heaven on "flowery beds of ease." But true prayer did not allow the Lord Jesus to do that, and neither will it allow us. You have leaped the hurdle of the will and have told your Lord, "Wherever You lead I'll go." Having offered yourselves, you are in for an adventure.

Sometimes the adventure is an intellectual one, as Pam and I found when we began to intercede for the Muslim world. Recognizing that we had a duty to pray for the one-fifth of the world's peoples behind the "Muslim curtain," we started a new page in our prayer notebook and set aside one day a week for intercession on their behalf. Spurred on in our faith by the incredible events that had happened in Eastern Europe and in the Soviet Union in 1989, we saw that God could break down seemingly impenetrable barriers.

But we soon realized that we knew only two missionary families residing in strongly Islamic nations, and were largely ignorant of how to pray in specifics. Yet the Spirit would not leave us alone; we could not ask Him for a Muslim breakthrough and remain largely in ignorance. As we took baby steps in praying for these people whom God loves as much as any people on earth, we became more alert to the sources within our reach that could help us learn about the Church's outreach to Islam.

The "Desert Storm" war in Kuwait and Iraq brought an explosion of information on the Arab world. Suddenly, TV and newspapers were full of facts and figures on Muslim people. We began to notice books on Muslim missions, and ordered two of them for ourselves. A magazine published by the U.S. Center for World Mission printed several stories on Muslim evangelism, including a map of Muslim populations, which went into our notebook. As we began to pray specifically for a couple in Turkey and another in Kenya, our church brought to our attention a missionary family entering Morocco and another going to Pakistan, and we have now begun receiving their prayer letters.

All of this is to say that when a couple gets serious about praying for others, they usually find themselves doing a lot more than praying. (Tom and Lisa have returned to Plano from Indonesia where they saw two members of Lisa's family confess Jesus as Lord.)

Accept One Another's Verbal Skills—Strong or Weak!

She writes . . .

Ruth, an Australian housewife and mother who knows the blessing of prayer with her husband, Mac, told Carey and me, "Praying should be as natural as eating." The trouble is, praying aloud does not *feel* natural to many people. A common stumblingblock to couple prayer is a feeling of awkwardness or embarrassment in the other's presence. A man whose wife never seems at a loss for words while praying can feel shy of trying—as can the wife of a super-articulate man.

Don and Helene Percy told us, "In the beginning we were self-conscious about our praying together out loud." But they found the solution in *acceptance.* "This self-consciousness no longer exists now that we both accept and are attentive to each other's prayers." They found that they needed to tell one another that each accepted the

other's prayers. By making a deliberate decision of acceptance, they freed each other of any need to impress the
partner.

My friend Martha Sandford says that she and Frank
found help early in their prayer life together through the
book *Conversational Prayer* by Rosalind Rinker. With practice it does become easier to voice one's concerns to God in
the presence of another, for that other person is not sitting
in judgment, but is a co-pleader, joining in with earnest
longing.

I let Carey know that I am with him in his praying by
sometimes uttering a soft "Yes, Lord" while he prays. A
whispered "Amen" from him lets me know that he is with
me in my petitions.

Carey and I, in fact, thoroughly enjoy words and trying
to express ourselves exactly. When I was first becoming
acquainted with Carey, I was delighted by his respect for
words and his use of them. I had prayed earlier that if the
Lord had a husband for me, one of his attributes would be
a love of words and of writing. During the five years of our
marriage I have watched Carey continue to enhance his
vocabulary. He tells me that it helps that he is an editor
with the good fortune of working with many fine writers.
How can deep truths be expressed, we sometimes wonder,
how can communication be maintained between man and
wife, and between a couple and their Creator, without the
means, the words, with which to do it adequately?

Carey and I make it an aim to learn words. We have a
daily tear-off calendar that introduces us to new terms. We
each keep a dictionary close by at all times—in our individual offices and on our desks at home. When we come
across a word we could not use in a sentence we look it up
and try to study its root meaning. We find it very reward-

ing to give thought to the meanings of words and thus to worship God as richly as our limited human language permits. But this is a personal preference and in no way earns us points with God! If He had given me an inarticulate husband, or Carey a less expressive wife, the key to our praying together would still be grateful acceptance of the other one's manner of expression.

Don't Presume It's the Woman's Place to Lead

Most of the couples who have shared their prayer histories with us agree that the wife is more likely to express a desire for prayer than the husband. My good friend Betsy Chapple, of Santa Ana, California, who shares in prayer with her husband, Jack, is representative of the women polled. "Prayer seems more important to the wife than the husband," she says, "for women are more dependent and security-minded; that is, they are less hesitant to admit their dependence and their needs in prayer than men."

Women also find intimacy easier to achieve than do men. Susan Winkleman, a friend of ours in Grand Prairie, says, "God, it seems, created women to speak 'the language of the heart.' They love to share their thoughts, feelings, goals and dreams." If this is true it is not hard to see why the wife is apt to initiate the prayer process in a given household.

Kathryn Railey suggests another reason why the woman may take the lead. "She is often the one who has continued with her faith development (going to church, Bible study, and such) whereas the husband may not have." There are certainly cases where the opposite is found, but in general

Kathryn's observation holds true. Is the wife then to take the driver's seat when it comes to prayer?

We would answer that ideally it should be the man as often as the woman. One husband who responded to our questionnaire wrote that men should not assume prayer is "women's work, or that it is foreign to manhood to pray." He offered the opinion that some men have a low view of prayer because they assume that God is like a busy executive, and that His business will roll on just fine without input from the rank and file.

We women may be more predisposed by our nature to pray and we may find prayer less threatening than do men. But, speaking as a woman, I am greatly helped by my husband's taking the lead. He has been the one to guide us into our form of structured prayer. And though I may actually lead in prayer as often as he on any given day, Carey is the one who maintains our prayer book and, most often, calls us to our daily prayer together. I am secure in this, and though I feel I could take the lead I am happier to follow.

Further, this reflects what I see in God's Word. There is a biblical principle that the husband has the responsibility for the spiritual development and religious training of the family, supported by the wife. In both the Old and New Testaments it is the man who is uniformly expected to serve as priest on behalf of his household.

Chuck Bianco says he finds it puzzling that women want to pray more than men, but the reason may be because of the intimacy required for couple prayer. He says, "It is so much easier to study Scripture than to expose your very being in front of your spouse. Many men find this risky. But it's what God wants. He wants us to go to Him, without pretense or protection. With a fifty percent divorce rate and so many parental failures I find it amazing that all men do not desire to pray with their wives."

Carey and I believe that in a marriage where the man and woman are equal partners, either one could be the prayer leader in much the same way as either one may be the primary breadwinner or the one who does the cooking. We really believe that the Holy Spirit should be the leader of husband-wife prayers and that He should be recognized as such by both marriage partners. In mutual submission to His holy guiding the man and woman can stand side by side in prayer to such a degree that it is difficult to tell who is the "leader."

Thus far we have looked at these factors that can endanger a lifetime of prayer with your partner: "good" things that distract you from the best, failure to "put feet to your prayers," undue concern about the words you use in praying, and the man's unwillingness to lead or support his wife as she leads. And there's another peril:

He writes . . .

Don't Allow Prayer Together to Take the Place of Individual Quiet Time

Neil, the salesman quoted in chapter 2, said in looking back on the breakdown of communication with Anne during his midlife crisis: "I wasn't spending time with God each day as I had done. . . ."

There is something even more important than praying with your wife or husband, and that's personal time with God daily. As strongly as Pam and I have come to believe in prayer together, we know that it cannot substitute for our own individual time with God. I thought of this Sunday when our pastor talked about prayer issuing from a continual attitude of walking with God. Formal prayer was of little use, he said, if the persons praying were not, in Brother Lawrence's words, "practicing the presence of God." Likewise it is true that prayer together, as husband and wife, depends for its vitality upon the personal, individual communion of each of them with God.

We believe we have never met a victorious believer who was not spending time daily with God in His Word and in prayer. For it is in the solitary place of seeking God that the soul feeds upon Christ and hears the Spirit's voice speaking personally to him or to her. So, the cautionary word here for each prayer partner is: *Keep your personal time with God.* For prayer to "work" in a couple's relationship, each marriage partner needs to maintain his or her walk as a good disciple—a "learner"—of Christ.

Don't Be Too Ambitious

This word of caution applies especially to couples just starting out to pray together. You probably feel slightly overwhelmed at the duty of responding to the needs in your own marriage, in the lives of friends and family, in your church and community, and in the world at large. Don't fall into the trap of trying to be God to all those in need. Start small!

Pam and I heard a Christian worker tell how he decided to pray for an hour every day. We were already beginning to feel guilty when he went on to say that when he had prayed for everything and everybody he knew to pray for, only seven minutes had passed. He immediately felt he was a failure, and so he did not pray at all the following day. Thankfully, he stayed with his original goal of praying daily, but he decided to spend only a few minutes at it each day at the beginning. He has now established a strong life of prayer that requires a half hour or more every day.

Years ago a man I remember from my training with the Navigators, Robert Foster, wrote a little tract called "Seven Minutes with God." It is about personal quiet time, but is equally relevant to prayer for couples. Bob Foster sought to get his readers to commit themselves to just seven minutes a day with God. He knew that would not be nearly enough time once the habit of prayer was formed!

We have suggested that you schedule two minutes a day for prayer together when you start out, and expand the time as you mutually agree on the need for it. Begin small and let your prayer life grow!

Beware of Legalism

In this book Pam and I may seem to come down hard for the idea of husbands and wives praying together. Even though we have tried not to let our own convictions run away with us, I fear that we have at times talked about prayer for couples as though it were one of the Ten Commandments. The last thing we want to do is lay a guilt trip on your prayer life—or lack thereof.

That is why we have inserted here and there little safety valve statements such as, "It's O.K. to miss your daily prayer time once in a while after you establish the habit," or, "If you can't keep your appointed time, don't feel you're a failure."

We have tried to say we are not to make prayer a little god. Prayer, which is a very desirable thing, should never be a burden. We have also tried to be transparent, allowing you to see that we too sometimes miss coming together for prayer—sometimes on purpose, to get needed rest and relief from schedules—and sometimes because of poor planning or forgetfulness. If you think you see some flexibility in our approach to prayer we will be glad. We want to avoid a legalism that would press the very life out of prayer.

A Dictionary of Theology defines *legalism* as "the idea that man's fulfillment of God's law is the indispensable foundation of man's standing with God." We have insisted that, on the contrary, our standing with God depends wholly upon His grace. The same dictionary defines *legalism* in ethics as "the idea that strict conformity to prescribed rules of conduct is the hallmark of moral goodness, even though the claims of compassion or even common sense are thereby inhibited." We are urging that you make the radical decision to pray each day together, but that you let common sense and compassion have full play. Jesus condemned none so thoroughly as He did those hypocrites who went about their religious practices in a rigid, self-righteous manner. And while He desires that we pray together often, the Lord Jesus did not Himself approach prayer as a duty. If we follow Him and go with the flow of the Holy Spirit's leading, we will find He is with us, blessing our praying, guiding our interceding, exulting in our praising. Where the Spirit of the Lord is there is liberty.

How do we know when we are becoming legalistic in our praying? When we are more concerned about spending a certain number of minutes in prayer than about the objects of our prayers. When the *form* of our prayers, such as the order in which we include adoration or supplication, is more important than the *content*. When spontaneity has vanished. When prayer becomes a burden. Remember Jesus' open-ended invitation,

Come to me, all you who are weary and burdened,
and I will give you rest. Take my yoke upon you and
learn from me, for I am gentle and humble in heart,
and you will find rest for your souls. For my yoke is
easy and my burden is light.   Matthew 11:28–30

Recognize Some "Tiredness" as Satan's Illusion

Honoring, as Jesus did, our legitimate needs for rest
and refreshment, we must at the same time be aware of
what we have come to think of as "imitation" fatigue. The
phenomenon of sudden sleepiness at prayer time is one
that every praying couple has to deal with. Tiredness, both
real and illusory, has always been a foe of prayer just as
good things have always been enemies of the best. The
three disciples who accompanied Jesus to Gethsemane the
night He was betrayed did our Lord little good. He asked
them to watch with Him in prayer, but they couldn't keep
their eyes open. From their disappointing behavior came
that convicting sentence, "The spirit is willing, but the flesh
is weak" (Matthew 26:41, NASB). How many of us could
write our names beside that!

Especially, it seems, when we come together to pray, a
strange drowsiness will settle upon us and neutralize our
efforts—unless we are prepared for it. We can combat
genuine fatigue by choosing a prayer time when both partners are apt to be most alert. Pam and I pray right after
supper because we know that later in the evening we may
be too sleepy.

But there's a kind of tiredness that has nothing to do
with our physical condition. Satan uses this simulated fatigue to discourage the saints from praying, allowing him

to go about his destructive business unhindered. Pam mentioned earlier that a "curious tiredness" often comes over us at prayer time. We now recognize that such tiredness may be devil-inspired, for Satan hates all prayer. When we sense this tiredness, we can also assume that among our prayer objectives for the evening is something the devil particularly doesn't want us to interfere with. So, we take fresh courage from God's promise to renew our strength (Isaiah 40:30–31) and we seek to pray all the more earnestly about the matters before us.

James and Shirley Dobson recall an incident when they had to overcome fatigue in order to pray. The dramatic results of their prayers have implications for us all. Here's Dr. Dobson's description of that evening.

> I'll never forget the time a few years ago when our daughter had just learned to drive. . . . It was during this era that Shirley and I covenanted between us to pray for our son and daughter at the close of every day. Not only were we concerned about the risk of an automobile accident, but we were also aware of so many other dangers that lurk out there in a city like Los Angeles. . . . That's one reason we found ourselves on our knees each evening, asking for divine protection for the teenagers whom we love so much.
>
> One night we were particularly tired and collapsed into bed without our benedictory prayer. We were almost asleep before Shirley's voice pierced the night. "Jim," she said. "We haven't prayed for our kids yet today."
>
> I admit it was very difficult for me to pull my 6'2" frame out of the warm bed that night. Nevertheless, we got on our knees and offered a prayer for our

children's safety, placing them in the hands of the Father once more.

Later we learned that [our daughter] Danae and a girl friend had gone to a fast-food establishment and bought hamburgers and Cokes. They drove up the road a few miles and were sitting in the car eating the meal when a policeman drove by, shining his spotlight in all directions, obviously looking for someone.

In a few minutes, Danae and her friend heard a "clunk" from under the car. They looked at one another nervously and felt another sharp bump. Then a man crawled out from under the car. He was unshaven and looked like he had been on the street for weeks. He tugged at the door attempting to open it. Thank God, it was locked. Danae quickly started the car and drove off . . . no doubt at record speed.

Later, when we checked the timing of this incident, we realized that Shirley and I had been on our knees at the precise moment of danger. Our prayers were answered. Our daughter and her friend were safe!*

The text at the beginning of this chapter reveals that there are times when no one is "standing in the gap" as an intercessor. As a result, God unleashes His judgment or Satan goes on stealing, killing and destroying (John 10:10).

What spiritual battles are you and your marriage partner up against that could be lost if you give in to tiredness and fail to stand in the gap? It is tragic that for so many who profess to be Christians, a serious commitment to pray seems an optional thing! Writing this book has driven Pam and me to the conclusion that everything God does He does in answer to prayer. Our sovereign God has or-

* James C. Dobson, *Love for a Lifetime* (Portland, Ore.: Multnomah Press, 1987), pp. 51–52.

dained that His children have a crucial role to play in the coming of His Kingdom.

Ezekiel was a prophet of the Exile, meaning that he served God in Babylon among the remnant of Judah that had been taken captive when Jerusalem was sacked in 586 B.C. In Ezekiel 22:30, God spoke to His remnant and told them part of the reason they had to go into exile and why their city and the Temple—where God communed with His chosen people—were destroyed. It was because *no one interceded for the Lord to spare His people.*

If this is a correct assessment of that historical set of circumstances, does it not serve to challenge us, in our apathy and unconcern, to wake up and consider our own circumstances? Should we not be diligent to "watch" with our God now and stand in the gap for our nation and for our world? The ease with which we let prayer slide, and succumb to slumber, should tell us a lot about how seriously we take the Scriptures. The Lord Jesus, and the New Testament writers, tell us plainly that this world is under God's judgment and is ripe for destruction. It is later than most of us think! Thus, we need to stay alert, on guard against Satan's subtle invitation to "sweet sleep."

For those who are willing to stand in the gap and pray, "Thy kingdom come, Thy will be done," there are promises. To those we turn in the next chapter.

10

The Promises: How to Get Answers from God

Thou art coming to a King,
Large petitions with thee bring;
For His grace and power are such,
None can ever ask too much.
John Newton (1725–1807)

"Call to me and I will answer you and tell you great
and unsearchable things you do not know."
Jeremiah 33:3

He writes . . .

God has made promises to His people. Peter called them
"exceeding great and precious promises" given to those
who believe in God through Christ (2 Peter 1:4, KJV).
When we pray as a couple we have two powerful truths
going for us. First, *God has promised to answer the prayers of
two who agree on the thing being asked.* Second, He has *made
specific promises* by which we can approach Him. By laying
hold of His promises we can know that we are praying in
line with God's will, and we can also know that He will
answer, for as a modern gospel song affirms, "my Re-
deemer is faithful and true."

Pam and I believe in this principle of praying God's promises into reality. As I mentioned earlier, we are holding certain verses in Psalm 90 before God, awaiting His answers for ourselves, for our work, and for my four children. In the five years since we have been claiming these promised blessings from the Lord in prayer, we have begun to see God work. Pam's ministry at Dallas Baptist University is a part of the fulfillment of what God promised. We believe that this book itself is another. "Yes, Lord," we pray, "establish the work of our hands."

For those answers still in the future, the testimony of Solomon encourages us to persevere in prayer. At the dedication of the Temple (1 Kings 8:56), he could say, "Praise be to the Lord, who has given rest to his people Israel just as he promised. Not one word has failed of all the good promises he gave through his servant Moses."

Someone has imagined arriving in his heavenly home and being taken by an angel into a large room filled with gifts in beautiful wrapping. The angel says, pointing to the great mound of presents, "Those are the gifts and blessings the Father had promised to you while you were on earth. But you never asked for them."

Though this is a mere story, it is certainly true that most Christians live far below their privilege as joint heirs with the Lord Jesus and children of the King. We need to encourage one another to begin to lay claim to all that God has for us—and not for our own happiness alone, but also for the good of others.

Pam and I do not set ourselves up as great examples, by any means, of living by the promises of God. But perhaps by sharing a few instances where we have actually stepped out on a promise and seen the result, we can encourage you to claim God's "good promises" in the challenges you yourself face. What joy to be able to say with the psalmist, "Your promises have been thoroughly tested, and your servant loves them" (Psalm 119:140).

Near my desk is a small stand-up plaque with these words of the prophet Jeremiah: " 'For I know the plans I have for you,' declares the Lord, 'plans to give you hope and a future"(Jeremiah 29:11).

This plaque means much to me for it was presented to me by our office prayer group when my job was eliminated in early 1991. Since February 1983 I had often carried in my shirt pocket a 3 x 5 card on which was this same verse from Jeremiah. I am looking at the card now; it is smudged and the corners are worn from much handling. Another card that has been handled so much that the printing is now almost too faint to read contains this promise: "If you have faith as a mustard seed, you shall say to this mountain, 'Move from here to there,' and it shall move; and nothing shall be impossible to you" (Matthew 17:20, NASB).

The card with the most rounded corners and stains, however, is one on which I typed some verses from Isaiah. Those verses contain a promise that lifted my hopes during that dark period in 1983 when all attempts at a reconciliation with my wife had failed. I was more alone than I ever had been, rooming in a large happy household where the celebration of life sometimes drove me deeper into my solitary, sad world. I had an old car and I well remember driving slowly "home" from work some days, lost in my blue mood. With all my savings gone and only weekend visits with one or more of the children, I was near defeat at times.

But I had maintained church attendance and the daily discipline of meeting the Lord for prayer and Scripture reading. One day I came upon these words in Isaiah 43:

> Remember not the former things, nor consider the things of old. Behold, I am doing a new thing; now it springs forth, do you not perceive it? I will make a way in the wilderness and rivers in the desert.
>
> Verses 18–19, RSV

Those statements, so far removed from me and my world, yet seemed to be God's word for me when I read them in 1983. I typed out the verses on a card and memorized them. Could the Lord be telling me also, as He told the children of Israel, to put my past behind me? Could I expect Him to do a "new thing" in my own life? I wondered.

Is a Scriptural Promise Ours to Claim?

I don't believe we can simply lay claim to any promise in the Bible, and so I hasten to add that I needed to take time to learn the meaning and understand the context of the passage before I could base my prayers on it. I could easily have thought, since the text contains a promise that I very much wanted to hear, that this had to be God's promise just for me, and consider the matter closed. But I needed to continue to listen to see if the Spirit was speaking through these verses to me in my situation. As I waited, the Spirit within me always cheered me when I meditated on this passage, and, gradually, I claimed the promise of the "new thing" that God was going to do, and began to look for evidence of newness springing up within my own world.

Samuel's experience in learning to recognize God's voice is apropos here. The child Samuel heard a voice speaking to him three times in the Temple in the still of the night (1 Samuel 3), but it was not until he checked this out with the elderly priest Eli that he knew that it was the Lord speaking to him. That is helpful for us today. When we think God is saying something to us, but we are not sure, we should seek counsel from someone more experienced in spiritual things. Such a person can help us discern the source of our "message."

Another guideline that can aid in determining whether or not a promise in Scripture is for us is to ask: Does this fit with what God is saying to me at this time from other passages of Scripture, from my own sense of the Spirit's leading and through my fellow believers?

Because I sometimes mark down a date in the margin beside a verse that I am claiming from the Lord, I can look back now and see other texts that were speaking to me at this time. For example, on April 30, 1983, I underlined this passage from Job 36:

> But those who suffer he delivers in their suffering;
>   he speaks to them in their affliction.
> He is wooing you from the jaws of distress
>   to a spacious place free from restriction,
>   to the comfort of your table laden with choice food.
> Verses 15–16

Beside those verses I wrote in the date, and "Yes, Lord, I now hear you. What bright promise for the future!"

On July 14 the following words especially impressed me:

> The moon will shine like the sun, and the sunlight will be seven times brighter, like the light of seven full days, when the Lord binds up the bruises of his people and heals the wounds he inflicted.   Isaiah 30:26

Beside that verse I wrote "I believe" and the date. Some six weeks later, on September 3, I made this notation beside Psalm 37: "There is no more room for fretting when we remember God is ours."

> Delight yourself in the Lord
>   and he will give you the desires of your heart.
> Commit your way to the Lord;
>   trust in him and he will do this: Verses 4–5

The text in Isaiah that promised a "new thing," then, was not an isolated thought. It was a part of the larger picture, a new trend in my thought life where hope was being nurtured and faith was building.

Did the "new thing" materialize? There were hopeful signs even amid my gloom in 1983. A mission society working in Romania made the decision that year to translate into Romanian three books of Sunday school lessons I had written, for use with the suffering Church. I cannot describe how this encouraged me. Another factor buoyed my emotions now and then; I was corresponding with a young woman who had proven a loyal friend, and strongly hoping for love to come back into my life.

In 1984 came another new development: I was asked by the mission to go to Romania in 1985 and teach lay leaders how to use my books in Bible classes. Such literature was illegal in Romania at that time, of course. I was to pose as a vacationer and do the teaching in clandestine, prearranged classes. The mission would make the arrangements. All I had to do was enter the country, show up at the gate of a certain church and then follow the directions of the local pastor. Oh, there was one other thing. I was to make sure no one followed me to the church!

I accepted this invitation and then saw God completely provide through churches, family and friends the $1,500 in expenses needed for the two-week trip. Toward the end of 1984, thinking of the forthcoming trip to Romania, I noted with unusual interest these words from 2 Corinthians 9, verse 8: "And God is able to make all grace abound to you, so that in all things at all times, having all that you need, you will abound in every good work." I wrote the date in the margin, 11/13/84, and added: "Thy promises I believe for the work You call me to."

God spoke encouragement to me through other means. Early in 1985 my help was asked with the writing of a book about China, *To Run and Not Be Weary,* by Stan Cottrell, and the extra earnings not only helped but the experience increased my confidence that God would supply all my need—whether wisdom, closeness to my children, money, emotional support, even a wife. That spring, however, my hopes for a love relationship with the young woman with whom I was corresponding were dashed when she informed me that to her I was "just a good friend." Yet even then God in His sovereign way provided comfort. On the way to the mailbox the day her letter arrived bearing the disappointing news, a song came to my mind that we sang at church. I was singing the words under my breath as I lifted the mail from the mailbox, affirming that "nothing I desire compares to You."

In May 1985 I went to Romania, where my faith was stretched as it had never been before. In Vienna, on my way into the country, a mission contact whose name I never was told gave me a map of Bucharest and told me to memorize the route from my hotel to the church, for once I was in the city, pulling out a map might attract the kind of help I did not want! At the Bucharest international airport I had to endure the searching scrutiny of the scowling security officer who checked my passport. I think he could not believe that I was vacationing in his country, then known for one of the world's most oppressive regimes.

In that and subsequent experiences, which threatened to frighten me while in Romania, I remembered a promise from the Bible given to me years earlier: "Do not fear, for I am with you; do not anxiously look about you, for I am your God. I will strengthen you, surely I will help you, surely I will uphold you with My righteous right hand" (Isaiah 41:10, NASB). My fears vanished when I came into the company of the Romanian believers, and I will always cherish the sense of God's powerful presence when worshipers filled the sanctuary on Saturday night for prayer and Sunday for worship.

One day in Oradea, in northern Romania, I returned to the church where I was to teach a class after having lunched with a brother, Constantin, who I later learned was a math teacher. All was quiet between us, for he knew no English and I knew only a few words in Romanian. The doors were locked at the church when we got there so we had to wait outside. Meanwhile, a small red car arrived and parked on the street nearby. The lone driver remained in the car. I was thinking about what I was going to teach in the class and was hardly conscious of the car.

Finally a woman came and unlocked the church door and we went in. Inside Constantin looked at me and put his hands to his eyes, cupping them as though he were peering through field glasses. Then he motioned over his shoulder, indicating that the man in the red car had been spying on us. Then he pointed toward heaven and again mimed looking through field glasses. He was telling me that the Father above was watching too, and that was what really mattered. This brought to my mind another of God's promises: "For the eyes of the Lord range throughout the earth to strengthen those whose hearts are fully committed to him" (2 Chronicles 16:9).

Upon returning home I was hoping soon to be able to move out of the small room where I had lived for almost three years, little knowing that in weeks I was not only going to move from there but out of the state and across the country into a new job. I was about to catch a fuller glimpse of the "new thing," which, rather lamely, at times, I was still expecting God to do.

In my first week back in the office, I was excited to receive an unsolicited job offer from a publisher in Texas. The company flew me to Waco where their offices were, and I liked what I saw. By July, having discussed the decision with Christian friends, including one of our church's pastors, and sensing a deep peace, I accepted the new job. A fellow housemate helped with the 1,600-mile drive west. Driving into Texas, which to me meant coming home after being away 22 years, I thought of how this state, with its vast expanses of arid land, is a sort of wilderness. And I remembered the words of Isaiah 43:19, "I will make a way in the wilderness," (RSV).

Six years after my coming to Texas, Pam and I are in the thick of that "new thing" God promised back in 1983. I have gone into some detail about this experience because it testifies to God's faithfulness to a very ordinary believer.

Rightly Interpreting a "Word from God"

One of the real tragedies in the church today is our saying that God has spoken, when He hasn't, or when we mistake the meaning of what He has said. I have always, until lately, admired the declaration, "The Bible said it, I believe it, that settles it!" But when someone says that today, I become nervous, for such a remark makes it appear that it is always a simple matter to understand the meaning of a given Scripture. To interpret God's Word aright often requires thought, study and time. Above all, it requires the Holy Spirit's illumination of the text.

Because Pam and I believe God does work and does fulfill His promises, we need to be careful in our own praying, and particularly in our reading of Scripture. In March 1895, George Muller of Bristol, England, wrote:

> I never remember, in all my Christian course, a period now of sixty-nine years and four months, that I ever sincerely and patiently sought to know the will of God by the teaching of the Holy Ghost, through the instrumentality of the word of God, but I have been always directed rightly. But if honesty of heart, and uprightness before God were lacking, or if I did not patiently wait upon God for instruction, or if I preferred the counsel of my fellow-men to the declarations of the word of the living God, I made great mistakes.

Note Muller's words of caution! Do you and I "sincerely" try "to know the will of God" by the Holy Spirit's teaching "through the instrumentality of the word of God"? Do we require of ourselves and our mates "honesty of heart" and "uprightness before God"? Do we know what it is to "patiently wait" for God's instruction, preferring it to the "counsel" of man? Searching questions, aren't they?

George Muller saw God supply the needs of his orphanage by one means only—prayer. Many examples of how he claimed the promises of God are given in the book *George Muller of Bristol.*

Other elements no doubt played a part in Muller's appropriation of God's promised blessings, but the feature that most impresses me is his habit of seeking God in the daily reading of Scripture. *The way* to get answers in prayer from God, he tells us, is to get to know God through regular study of His Word. Those husbands and wives who individually and daily expose themselves to the Bible find themselves able, more and more, to pray according to God's will and receive answers to their prayers. Pam recalls the prayer life of Corrie ten Boom.

She writes . . .

Corrie began her day with the Bible. When I took her a cup of tea early in the morning I would often find her with her beloved Phillips version of the New Testament resting on her chest, her clear blue eyes twinkling with the ideas she had been talking over with her God. I knew that she was looking to Him always for His promises. Brother Andrew also recalls her absolute trust in the promises found in His Word. In his book *And God Changed His Mind* he alludes to Corrie's habit of quoting the Bible back to the Lord as a way of reminding Him of His promises:

> She would have made a great lawyer. When she grew especially impassioned, she would grab her Bible and thumb through the pages rapidly until she found the exact passage she could use to prove her case. Then she would lift her Bible into the air, point to the verse and say triumphantly, "Here, Lort [she always pronounced it "Lort"]—read it Yourself."

Three Promises

Many couples have written to Carey and me quoting Matthew 18:20 as the primary scriptural grounds for husband-wife prayers. Pat Bianco, for example, wrote that "the promise 'Wherever two or more are gathered in my name, I am there' took on special significance for us as a married couple after we realized that our prayer life and spirituality were meant to be shared." Gail and Dennis Linam told us that "praying together taps the scriptural promise 'where two or three are gathered in my name.' We expect God to hear and answer our prayers of faith because He has promised."

Notice the emphasis on this verse as a *promise*. This suggests a rather obvious way to apply the principle of "standing on the promises of God" in our praying. We can begin by saying aloud the verse and responding in some such way as this: "Loving Father, we come to You now as two of Your children. Thank You for Your presence here with us, as You have promised. Praise Your holy name! We pray today for. . . ."

Then there are the promise-filled words of Acts 16:31: "Believe in the Lord Jesus, and you will be saved—you and your household" (RSV).

This double-barreled promise—*you* will be saved, and *your family*—was given to their jailer by the apostle Paul and his co-worker Silas. And indeed not only did the jailer turn to Christ and receive salvation, but his whole household did as well. Rightly understood, this verse shows that God will sometimes save one member of a family and then systematically bring all of the other family members to faith because of that first one's obedience. While other Scriptures show that receiving Christ may divide a family

(Matthew 10:34–37), this passage encourages us to believe God will save entire families.

Do you have unsaved family members for whom you are praying? Acts 16:31 is a strong promise on which to take your stand and plead with God for their eternal salvation.

A third example of a scriptural promise was pointed out to us recently when Carey and I were visiting the Waco home of Charles and Dorothy Shellenberger, who were responsible, in the plan of God, for introducing us to each other in 1986. They are a couple who continually demonstrate the principle of claiming promised blessings from God.

Now retired, the parents of four grown children and eleven grandchildren, they are not resting on their considerable laurels. They live disciplined lives and are very much "in the heat of the battle" for God and righteousness. A typical comment of Charles: "For our children and each grandchild we are claiming this promise from Philippians: 'I am confident of this very thing, that He who began a good work in you will perfect it until the day of Christ Jesus' " (1:6, NASB). Dorothy added: "When we pray for one of the family, we put that name in the verse. 'I am confident that He who began a good work in Sally (or David or Richard or Susan) will perfect it.' " With some frequency they remind the Lord of this promise that they are claiming from His Word. They are "standing on the promises," as the hymnist Kelso Carter declared:

> Standing on the promises that cannot fail,
> When the howling storms of doubt and fear assail,
> By the living Word of God I shall prevail,
> Standing on the promises of God.

Writing It Down

Finally, in claiming a promise in prayer, we find it help-ful to keep some kind of written record. Unless we write it down, we may forget that at one time God spoke to us very personally through one of His promises.

If you are using a prayer journal, that is a good place for such a record. We use our prayer notebook in this way. On the various pages—sometimes for our own needs, some-times for a missionary, a friend or someone who needs to come to know the Lord—we have recorded the promise we are standing on.

I wish we had been more consistent in doing this, but we do have some record of how a promise from God provided the content of our praying.

The couples we have polled have usually named "guid-ance" as one of the chief things for which they pray. The same is true for Carey and me. Probably the most crucial need for guidance we have felt in our married life came in 1988 when Carey's employer moved us to the Dallas met-ropolitan area. Thankfully, our little house in Waco had sold and we were able to consider buying another house. But where in the sprawling metroplex should we start looking? A dozen suburbs and communities in the area looked viable. Had money been no object, the choices would have been that much more confusing! Carey and I made a list of the things we wanted in a house:

—Safety and quiet
—Proximity to work
—Four bedrooms, or the equivalent
—Lots of light
—A small, private yard
—Within our budget!
—Near a gym and post office

As our house search stretched on and on we claimed Psalm 32:8 and a paraphrase of that verse went in our prayer notebook: "Father, we thank You that You instruct us and guide us in the way we should go and direct us with Your eye."

Actually we were getting a little panicky. Already we had put $1,000 down on one house and then withdrawn our offer, having a lack of peace about its location. Our lease on our small Dallas apartment would be up in March, but we hated even to wait that long because Jim and Carey and I were doing little more than "camping out" there. Then it happened. It was Monday, November 28, when we claimed Psalm 32:8 in prayer together. On Friday of that week, December 2, the Lord guided us to a model home that stood invitingly in southern Grand Prairie. We brought in our realtor on Sunday and by nightfall the deal was done. Carey wrote in our notebook: "A new home in G. Prairie."

"Safety and quiet" were the first things on our list of features desired in a house. What about the other items on that list? As for "proximity to work," the house is only twelve minutes' drive from our offices. Also, we got the equivalent of four bedrooms, and anyone visiting us would attest to the fact that our house has "lots of light." That it be "near a gym and a post office" were not really requirements. We could easily have done without those. But wouldn't you know! When we began to explore our new neighborhood we found a fitness gymnasium only five minutes to the north and a brand new post office opening up about a mile to the south. It seems God must have been looking over our shoulders when we wrote out our list.

In January, when we moved in we must have been reading in the minor prophets for there is an unusual reference in our notebook on January 6. It is Zephaniah 3:13, which surprises us now as we look back at it, for we do not remember ever hearing God speak from that obscure book. It was another promise: "They will eat and lie down and no one will make them afraid." We can say now, four years later, *true!*

Writing down what you are asking in faith is a small sign of your commitment. It says, "We are appropriating this particular passage—unless and until God guides us otherwise—for thus and so." As you continue to stand upon the promise and pray, you can add other dates and record how your prayer is changing, and how you see God answering your supplication. Looking back now at some of those records stimulates Carey and me to have faith for objectives and goals yet to be realized.

How to Claim a Promise

These then are steps to take in receiving answers from God:

1. Seek to know God by regular individual reading, study and meditation in the Word. Memorization aids in this. Read authors who know God and His Word, and take advantage of what they have learned in areas that interest you, such as parenting or stewardship of money.
2. Pray individually for God to teach you by His Spirit. Pray for your leaders in the Lord—your pastor, your Bible teacher—that God will speak through them.
3. Pray with your wife or husband for God to show you His will in specific matters. Ask Him to teach you both how to pray.
4. Ask Him to give you a promise to claim for specific needs. Then watch for Him to do that.

5. Continue to pray, adopting the attitude of a servant who is awaiting the master's word. Be teachable, open, willing to change what you think, so that the Spirit can lead you in truth.

6 Share with other praying people what you are praying for so they can join with you.

7. Share with these same people the answers God gives to encourage them in their own prayers. The more of us who know of what God has done, the stronger is His Church to pray.

8 Write down the promises God has given you and persevere in claiming them. Continue to listen for His promises for tomorrow!

11

And Don't Forget to Praise Him!

First worship God.
  He that forgets to pray
Bids not himself good-morrow
  Or good-day.
                Thomas Randolph (1523–1590)

> But you are a chosen people, a royal priesthood, a
> holy nation, a people belonging to God, that you may
> declare the praises of him who called you out of dark-
> ness into his wonderful light.   1 Peter 2:9

He writes . . .

Why a chapter wholly devoted to praise in a book about
prayer for couples? Pam and I would have asked the same,
until we read the responses to one of the questions in our
survey: "When you pray together, what are the elements
of your prayers? Confession, thanksgiving, intercession?"

Each couple answered that question a little differently,
but all, without exception, named "intercession" as a constant in their prayer life. Adoration, or praise, the "A" of
ACTS praying, was mentioned by less than half. Perhaps
we were at fault by the way we phrased the question, but

the results suggest a sadly overlooked element. Prayer, to most of us, is conversation with God in which we ask for what we and others need. And that is perfectly O.K. God wants us to do this. We have it from the lips of Jesus: "Ask and it will be given to you; seek and you will find; knock and the door will be opened to you" (Matthew 7:7). But God deserves more than supplications; real prayer requires more. Precisely, prayer requires the lovely element of praise.

What is praise? Why is it so important? Why does the Bible, in one place, speak of it as a "sacrifice"? How do you offer praise in a meaningful way? What are the benefits of praise to the ones praying? In this chapter we want to consider this most-neglected aspect of praying.

Why Praise?

Holy Scripture teaches us to offer praise to God. "Ascribe to the Lord the glory due to His name; worship the Lord in holy array" (Psalm 29:2, NASB). For the word *praises* in 1 Peter 2:9, the Amplified Bible has "that you may *set forth the wonderful deeds and display the virtues and perfections* of Him Who called you out of darkness." Thomas Kelly said, in the words of a favorite hymn:

> Praise the Savior, ye who know Him!
> Who can tell how much we owe Him?
> Gladly let us render to Him
> All we are and have.

Praise is due the Lord for who He is and for all He has done. And when we come together in prayer, it is right and good that first, before all else, we render up to God this that is due. Pam has said to me that as a British subject she would not think of going casually into the presence of the Queen. And we should not enter God's presence without acknowledging His majesty.

Earlier we have said that true prayer is precisely that: coming into His presence. Do we truly know what it is to come into God's presence in our prayer time? We asked other couples: "What do you think is the most important goal of prayer together?" One couple, with long experience in prayer, answered, "acknowledgment of God's person, presence and sovereignty in everything that has to do with us, our loved ones, our work and the world."

This, then, seems the place for prayer to begin. For Pam and me, we find that this usually calls for moments of quiet at the start of our prayers together. In those moments we are directing the focus of our whole united being as wife and husband upon God. We do not always read a Scripture portion, but often we do in order to fix our minds on the Lord and His Kingdom and to leave—for a time—the many cares of the day. We are acknowledging God's person, His presence and His lordship.

A song or hymn helps. Pam and I enjoy singing, and often open the hymnal and sing before praying. If you two do not sing, it may help you, at times, to praise God by listening to a recorded song of adoration and then using those words in your opening prayers.

At this beginning moment, one of us begins to pray aloud, offering a "sacrifice of praise." Praise, according to the dictionary, is "the act of expressing approval or admiration." It is "commendation . . . offering of grateful homage in words or song, as an act of worship." Synonyms for *praise* are "acclamation, plaudit, applause, approbation.

compliment." *Applause* and *compliment* are everyday words and it helps to think of praise in those familiar terms.

The writer to the Hebrews said: "Through Jesus, therefore, let us continually offer to God a sacrifice of praise—the fruit of lips that confess his name" (Hebrews 13:15).

Praising God may be seen as a "sacrifice" for it is costly. Just the act of turning the heart toward God and His Kingdom means that, for a little while, we turn away from whatever ordinarily fills our minds, whether it be the stock market, ironing, sports, food, hobbies—even sickness and sorrow. If God is the sovereign Lord, then it is right to sacrifice our preoccupations in acknowledging Him. But this, according to the Hebrews verse, means more than a mental nod. It involves "the fruit of lips." So, in the beginning of our prayer time, having directed our souls' focus to the Father, we further offer a sacrifice of praise by telling God with our mouths what we think of Him, by complimenting and applauding Him with our spoken words. This obviously requires effort, and that is a part of the "sacrifice" also.

To praise God is to tell Him what we think of Him. This allows us to speak of His "wonderful deeds" and of His "virtues and perfections." The poets and song writers have waxed ever so eloquently in this department; their words seem to match His majestic character. And by reciting their phrases—such as suggested in chapter 8—we can learn to praise Him in accord with His exalted place. But we need not wait to praise God until we have acquired "flowery' language. He will accept the adoration of the most fumbling tongue, if offered from the heart.

For those just starting to pray as a couple, committing no more than two minutes a day to this discipline, the opening of Jesus' model prayer is a good way to begin

Both husband and wife can say aloud, "Our Father, who art in heaven, hallowed be Thy name." Whatever our words, the goal in praise is to acknowledge who God is. As you spend longer in prayer together, you will discover more language with which to extol Him, but you will never outgrow the insights of the model prayer.

Our friend Eng Go describes the role it plays for him:

> When I prayed that the Lord would teach me how to have a dynamic prayer life, the answer was found in the Lord's Prayer. In my Bible, the New International Version, the prayer starts with the word *Father* all by itself on the first line. I thought how when I pray I usually call to the Father, but I was not sure what kind of Father I was calling to. As I thought about that single word, I found the name *Father* taking on different and awesome attributes of God almighty. Then I realized the beauty and aroma of prayer.
>
> After I truly, absolutely and surely know whom I am calling to and with whom I am having conversation—what kind of a Father He is—then I realize and am overwhelmed with His presence: "Hallowed be thy Name." It is awesome to be able to acknowledge His presence—so wonderful, so peaceful, so secure. And once I am overwhelmed with His presence and holiness, I understand something of what eternity means and what His Kingdom is all about. At this point I am up there with the Father in His presence looking at this world from the perspective of His Kingdom. Then the Lord sort of takes me down to earth to once again feel and understand the reality of earth—my needs, the needs of others, my wrongdoings, my relationship with others—but now with a heavenly perspective.

To Know Him Is to Praise Him

We are defining prayer as knowing God. Praise is an inevitable consequence of getting to know Him. To know God is to praise Him!

Praise is the purest form of prayer. Perhaps this is another reason why it is called "a sacrifice," for when we praise God we are not trying to obtain anything from Him. We are worshiping Him for who He is and dwelling upon His attributes.

But like everything that God requires of us, the commandment to praise Him is not just for His benefit, but also for ours. We can never outgive God! Three benefits at least come to those who praise. The first is *the manifest presence of God.* We have already noted that two who pray together have the promise of God's presence (Matthew 18:20). Psalm 22:3 offers a vivid image of this: "Yet Thou art holy, O Thou who art enthroned upon the praises of Israel" (NASB).

The *Hastings Dictionary of the Bible* says that the idea here is "that the praises, ascending like clouds of incense, form, as it were, the throne upon which Jehovah sits." You may be more familiar with the King James language: "O thou who inhabitest the praises of Israel." This verse encourages us to believe that where praise is, there God dwells in a special sense. If you want to know God's presence as you pray together, offer Him praises, and take by faith this promise that He will make His habitation with you.

A second benefit occurs in the realm of the emotions. Pam and I have come to recognize that by praising God *the human spirit is lifted.* Since we come together for prayer in the evening, we often start out feeling tired. The day's mail waiting for us at home sometimes contains disappoint-

ments. Many evenings we would sooner relax than keep
our prayer time. But if we begin to praise God by sheer
willpower, His Spirit lifts our spirits. We feel renewed and
find ourselves talking to the Father with fresh energy
about the intercessory needs of the day. We should be
willing to praise Him even without this emotional uplift,
but it seems to happen without exception that when we
praise and look to Him, joy and strength, resolution and
refreshment are given to us.

A third benefit, also promised in Scripture, is that praise
leads to victory. Second Chronicles 20 records a battle between King Jehoshaphat and Judah on the one hand, and
three of their most fearsome enemies on the other. Learning that "a vast army" was on its way, people streamed
from every town in Judah to Jerusalem to see if God would
come to their rescue. King Jehoshaphat stood in the assembly and began to praise the Lord. Watch how he com-
pliments and applauds Jehovah:

> "O Lord, God of our fathers, are you not the God
> who is in heaven? You rule over all the kingdoms of
> the nations. Power and might are in your hand, and
> no one can withstand you."   Verse 6

In prayer he traces the history of Israel with their foes, so
as to remind himself of the "wonderful deeds" of the Lord.
"We do not know what to do," he concludes, "but our eyes
are upon you [God]."

The people stood still when the king finished, and then
a Levite spoke out as "the Spirit of the Lord came upon"
him. He said, "Do not be afraid or discouraged because of
this vast army. For the battle is not yours, but God's." He
then gave instructions, which the king followed. The fol-

lowing morning Jehoshaphat "appointed men to sing to the Lord and to praise him for the splendor of his holiness as they went out at the head of the army, saying: 'Give thanks to the Lord, for his love endures forever.' " Verse 22 reports the outcome: "As they began to sing and praise, the Lord set ambushes against the men of Ammon and Moab and Mount Seir . . . and they were defeated."

Victory for the people of God came as they sang and praised the Lord. Such stories as this are preserved in the Bible for "our instruction, that through perseverance and the encouragement of the Scriptures we might have hope" (Romans 15:4, NASB). We, too, encounter situations in which we ourselves can do nothing. That is when God is saying to us: praise Me! When we do, He will win the victory.

In closing this chapter, we need to say two more things. First, choose a *place* to pray that will allow the full expression both of praise and of emotion. Sometimes, your hearts will be so crushed that you will want to cry. At other times, you will be so filled with joy and victory that you will still need to cry—but your cry will be one of praise. The primary Hebrew word for *praise* in the Old Testament means to "break out in a cry." If God has given you a victory, it's all right to shout about it!

Second, it is true that the Church today is facing fearsome enemies. It should be obvious that our current level of spiritual warfare is inadequate. To take one example alone, as a couple we have been standing in prayer against the rise of homicide in Dallas County where we live. But last year the city set a new record of 500 homicides. Our praying, and the prayers of others in this region, have not been enough to bind Satan and change this great evil. What if God's people, two by two, as couples and as prayer partners and as churches all over this metropolitan area looked to 2 Chronicles 20:20 as a model and took to praising God and extolling the Lord God for His "virtues and perfections"? Would He not guide us to a more concerted effort against evil—to put feet to our prayers—and would He not give us victory? Would He not answer His people for Los Angeles, for Washington, D.C., for Houston, for London, for New York and for your city if we humbled ourselves before Him and called upon Him as did Jehoshaphat? "Lord, we do not know what to do. Our eyes are upon You."

> Praise the Lord.
> Praise the Lord from the heavens,
>   praise him in the heights above. . . .
> Praise the Lord from the earth,
>   you great sea creatures and all ocean depths,
> lightning and hail, snow and clouds,
>   stormy winds that do his bidding,
> you mountains and all hills,
>   fruit trees and all cedars,
> wild animals and all cattle,
>   small creatures and flying birds,
> kings of the earth and all nations,
>   you princes and all rulers on earth,
> young men and maidens,
>   old men and children.
> Let them praise the name of the Lord,
>   for his name alone is exalted;
>   his splendor is above the earth and the heavens.
>   Psalm 148:1–2, 7–13

12

Praying Together: Guardian of Intimacy

> "Haven't you read . . . that at the beginning the Creator 'made them male and female,' and said, 'For this reason a man will leave his father and mother and be united to his wife, and the two will become one flesh'?"
>
> Matthew 19:4–5

He writes . . .

The intimate marriage was God's idea. It wasn't the creation of Madison Avenue, nor was it given to the world by marriage therapists. No, the intimate marriage union is as old as mankind.

When God came in the Person of Jesus and got involved in "our world"—as we in our pride like to think of it—He declared God's original intention for marital intimacy. In answer to those who questioned Him about divorce and remarriage Jesus, in the quote above, referred His questioners—and us—back to the beginning.

Yet the idea that intimacy in marriage can be attained appears impossible to many today. Pam and I are not trained in the dynamics of interpersonal relationships—that complicated arena!—and so we tread into this subject with the caution of a long-tailed pussycat in a room full of rocking chairs!

A Three-Ply Cord

Our conviction that intimacy is vital to this topic of prayer was confirmed when other couples, describing their experience of praying together, proceeded naturally to its significance in the marriage relationship. They described the goal of their prayer life variously as: "to stay close to God and each other," "intimacy with God and each other," "to become one," "openness, trust, listening, sensitivity."

David and Jeanette Bassett wrote: "We both feel that communication with God deepens . . . the spiritual and emotional intimacy we share with one another. Prayer is the means by which we build upon the Lord's love for us as the foundation of our marriage, and the medium by which we achieve spiritual agreement (Amos 3:3). The goal of our prayer life is spiritual unity, emotional oneness and marital harmony."

"Sharing our spiritual lives," said Joel and Maria Shuler, "is one of the ways we work at being truly intimate. We believe that God wants us to be one, to be united in every way possible. Our total couple intimacy is enhanced by our couple prayer. When we listen in to each other's private conversation with God, we are at our most vulnerable. It is a gift we give to each other, a special time." This is from a couple who found praying together "awkward" at first.

Joel and Maria are Catholics and have been committed to prayer together since Joe's conversion from Judaism some ten years ago. "At first," they recall, "we had to pray mostly traditional prayers" from a book, but Maria knew them so well she would run ahead of Joel. At one point their inability to pray at the same pace struck them as very funny. "We laughed so hard we couldn't continue with the prayer, but the experience freed us up to be more comfortable and natural before the Lord," Maria says.

Nancy and Bob Mapes told us, "We feel free to share whatever is going on with us, although we may not always do so for various reasons." Intimacy, in other words, does not place demands on either marriage partner to "tell all." Both share voluntarily, knowing that whatever is revealed will be accepted because they trust one another.

"Spiritual intimacy is a very important part of our marriage," said Pat Bianco. She went on:

> We believe that God wants us to be united in mind, heart and body. We work toward unity in every area of our lives, and have much to glean when we share our faith and spirituality with each other. We see how we complement and learn from each other, and thank God for bringing us together. God, Chuck and I are like a three-ply cord that is woven and intertwined.

In an article entitled "How Do You Build Intimacy in an Age of Divorce?" writer Caryl S. Avery noted:

> Given one wish in life, most people would wish to be loved—to be able to reveal themselves entirely to another human being and be embraced, caressed, by that acceptance. People who have successfully built an intimate relationship know its power and comfort. But they also know that taking the emotional risks that allow intimacy to happen isn't easy. . . . Intimacy requires consummate trust. And today trust is in short supply.*

Two truths struck me in Ms. Avery's statement. First, her reference to intimacy as something that must be *built*. Pam and I have certainly found this to be true.

---

* Caryl S. Avery, "How Do You Build Intimacy in an Age of Divorce?," *Psychology Today*, May 1989, pp. 27–31.

When we were becoming friends, in the first weeks of our relationship, we could not share the intimate secrets of our lives. Cautiously and tentatively, as the days passed, we revealed more of ourselves. After knowing each other three weeks, during which time we were together often, I took a sizeable risk with Pam. We were driving back from Dallas to Waco on a rainy night, which gave me an excuse to slow down a bit to prolong the journey and allow for the most personal sharing we had known up to that time. That was the night I mustered up the courage to tell Pam about the breakup of my first marriage for I wanted her to know what had happened and I especially hoped that she might agree with me that my circumstances did not prevent remarriage. She listened quietly. And then, as objectively as I knew how, I broached the subject of marriage. Would she consider marriage at all, I asked, or was she committed to the single life.

It surprises me to look back on that night and realize what deep waters I was moving into, for neither of us had overtly expressed how we were feeling toward one another. And I certainly was not working up to a proposal! I just wanted to know if these good vibrations I was getting whenever I thought of her could eventually mean anything!

Because she showed that she understood about my divorce and because marriage for her was an option within God's will, I was eager to return the next day for one last brief visit before she departed for California. Our taking some risks in conversation the night before had brought us much closer together. We were now able to hold hands and pray together.

As soon as Pam arrived in California I took another risk: I phoned to see if she had arrived safely, secretly wanting to maintain the closeness I felt we had "built." As the weeks went by I looked forward to her frequent letters and to our weekly long-distance calls.

At one point I evidently was concerned lest in my letters I was coming on too fast. Pam wrote back:

> . . . Your letter of Saturday arrived this afternoon and you told me to tell you if I felt uncomfortable with the way you are expressing yourself. Surprised as I am with my own reaction I must tell you that I don't feel uncomfortable, nor dishonest in the response of my heart and I do experience the peace of the Lord. As busy as life is (for both of us) it would be understandable to stop thinking of you, yet I find that I do not, nor do I want to.

I still remember when Pam wrote and asked me my age. And I recall asking her in a letter how she preferred being addressed. Men don't know any more what is proper etiquette. Did she want to be called "Miss?" "Ms."? Simply "Pam"? Then I took a flight of half-serious whimsy and asked, "Or do you prefer Mrs.?"

Pam responded rather matter of factly that she did not like "Ms." We kept sharing more of ourselves. In early March, a month after she had returned to California, Pam wrote:

> . . . I too like to take mental journeys through the weeks of our relationship. Did you know that you have very expressive eyes? I noticed them the evening we met. And the way you welcomed me to your home the afternoon after our walk was significant to me in our friendship. Yes I think you are right that our feelings have become stronger just recently. I know

that mine have. I find it very hard to be away from you. I long for your letters and to hear your voice. Yet, as we said on Friday, this time must be for our good. That verse—Psalm 84:11b—has been much on my mind lately. It happens very often, does it not, that we find ourselves thinking along the same lines. I find it intriguing that we have so many things in common and know many of the same people and places. More than that, it seems our souls have a similar heartbeat. Am I mistaken? Is that fanciful?

In a short while we had become what Christian psychologist Gary Collins describes as "intimate friends"—people who "understand each other and experience a closeness, acceptance, loyalty, vulnerability, accountability, caring, empathy and love that is not present in mere friendship."*

Sometime after we began our coveted weekly telephone trysts, I found myself giving Pam a blessing as we ended our conversation. I don't remember how the idea occurred to me; I wasn't in the habit of doing it. I can only conclude that the Spirit led me. I would pray for her, sometimes in the words of the old Hebrew blessing: "The Lord bless you and keep you; the Lord make His face shine upon you and be gracious to you; the Lord lift up His countenance upon you and give you peace." Or I would suit my prayer of blessing to her particular circumstances for the coming week. Because Pam showed such genuine appreciation of this, I would give her a blessing at the end of almost every phone call. I mention it here because it seems to indicate that prayer was being used of God to cement our fledgling relationship.

* Gary R. Collins, *Christian Counseling*, revised ed. (Word: Dallas, 1988), p. 189.

As intimate friends Pam and I were far from having an intimate relationship. That required more time, especially more time together, before and especially after the wedding, as day by day—in the physical, spiritual, emotional and intellectual realms—we "built" intimacy and gained "emotional safety" with each other.

The second truth that stands out in Ms. Avery's article is that "consummate trust" is the stuff of which intimacy is made. Couples who share in an intimate marriage have not gained that precious closeness through luck or "good genes." They have acquired it through taking risks with each other, with "the four walls down and the roof off," as a friend used to say in speaking of the transparency required in intimacy.

As children, most of us trusted everyone. But life soon taught us that this was a mistake. To achieve an intimate marriage, each partner has to put behind him past experiences of disappointment and betrayal. We believe that Christ Jesus, by His indwelling Spirit, can heal these memories and assist the believer in regaining that childlike openness. Given time, the Christian possesses an enormous advantage over the unbeliever when it comes to developing the ability to trust another person, and become worthy of trust. (We're not speaking, of course, of cases in which a personality disorder or mental illness obstructs a person's progress.) We ourselves, by the Spirit's enabling, can become more trustworthy; and trusting God, we can learn to trust another human being.

And basic to the Christian's "equipment" in this process is a life of prayer. Pam's close friend, Betsy Chapple, said in response to our questionnaire that "praying together gives a different level of bonding to a couple than they can experience through everyday activities." Kathy Bruner remarked, "I can't imagine *any* intimacy at all if we were not intimate in the deepest of issues."

Ken and Brenda Barker told us, "The most important goal of prayer together is that it keeps our relationship as a couple intimate and close, and it keeps our hearts open before the Lord as a couple. There is a lot of unspoken accountability in our walk with the Lord and with each other. We don't usually think of it in those terms, but ultimately that is what happens."

Christian couples who have the most intimate marriages have often proved to have this in common—a daily prayer life. This suggests to us that prayer between marriage partners serves as the keeper and guardian of intimacy. It introduces, as the Barkers say, an element of "accountability" to one another.

Since we began writing this book a marriage that Pam and I had thought unassailable has been ripped open by an affair. Ian (not the husband's real name) was a Christian minister, the father of four children. The woman involved with him was the church secretary and a mother. Pam and I had spent our vacation with Ian and his wife, "Mary," a year earlier. Was this incredible news really true? Pam knows Mary very well, and after receiving the news she recalled a recent conversation with Mary in which she had told Pam, "Ian and I pray together only a couple of minutes a day now, much less than we once did."

Prayer, of course, cannot take the place of conversation and affection and acts of kindness, and a thousand other little things that make up a healthy relationship.* But had

* Pam and I discovered recently a helpful book, *The Language of Love* by Gary Smalley and John Trent. Their discussion of the use of "emotional word-pictures" to maximize intimacy and understanding may be helpful to couples struggling with communication.

For our deliverance from all affliction, wrath,
   danger and necessity, we pray to the Lord.
Lord, have mercy.
Help us, save us, have mercy on us, and keep us, O
   God, by Your grace.
Lord, have mercy.

"Real Tenderness"

"In marriage, intimacy includes sexuality," notes Gary
Collins. "But it should not be assumed that all intimacy
involves sex.* Sex nevertheless was ranked high among
the aspects of intimacy prized by praying couples. Wrote
one wife: "There is a real tenderness when we pray together." Some couples reported that "passion" is one thing
they ask from God. All of them revealed a healthy, whole
view of sexuality. If in our day the prize of satisfying,
wonderful sex is a thing greatly desired—and it is without
question—these couples have found it, in the committed,
monogamous, prayerful, intimate marriage.

As we were completing the writing of this manuscript,
Newsweek magazine devoted its cover story to prayer. The
writers reported this same strong tie between prayer and
intimacy, stating that surveys by the sociologist-writer Andrew Greeley "show that spouses who pray together report
greater marital satisfaction than those who don't, and that
frequent sex coupled with frequent prayer make for the
most satisfying marriages."†

The husband we interviewed wrote: "My wife and I consider our sexual intimacy to be an area of prayer. We pray
... each time we make love, we will fall more deeply in

*_____s, *Christian Counseling,* p. 190.
†_____ng to God," *Newsweek* (January 6, 1992) 119:1, p. 41.

our friends been praying together and opening their hearts to God before one another, there would not have been any room for a "stranger" in either of their lives. As one couple told us: "We are each other's spiritual sounding board and counselor."

Daily prayer can serve as the guardian of the marriage, for the husband and wife who pray together do not pray alone. God Himself is present and He will not tolerate any duplicity. He will, on the other hand, encourage the formation of an ever-closer bond and He will lend His strength to that bond so that nothing can break it.

The Orthodox Church in America has, in its Ceremony of Matrimony, a carefully worded litany that points toward intimacy. The Reverend David Ford of St. Tikhon's Seminary in South Canaan, Pennsylvania, shared it with us; we have used it in our prayer time. It is especially appropriate on an anniversary. We have taken the liberty adapting the wording slightly:

> That You will send down upon us perfect and peaceful love, and assistance, we pray to the Lord.
> Lord, have mercy.
> That You will preserve us in oneness of mind in steadfast faith, we pray to the Lord.
> Lord, have mercy.
> That you will preserve us in a blameless life, we pray to the Lord.
> Lord, have mercy.
> That the Lord our God will grant us an honorable marriage and a bed undefiled, we pray to the Lord.
> Lord, have mercy.

For our deliverance from all affliction, wrath,
   danger and necessity, we pray to the Lord.
Lord, have mercy.
Help us, save us, have mercy on us, and keep us, O
   God, by Your grace.
Lord, have mercy.

"Real Tenderness"

"In marriage, intimacy includes sexuality," notes Gary
Collins. "But it should not be assumed that all intimacy
involves sex.* Sex nevertheless was ranked high among
the aspects of intimacy prized by praying couples. Wrote
one wife: "There is a real tenderness when we pray together." Some couples reported that "passion" is one thing
they ask from God. All of them revealed a healthy, whole
view of sexuality. If in our day the prize of satisfying,
wonderful sex is a thing greatly desired—and it is without
question—these couples have found it, in the committed,
monogamous, prayerful, intimate marriage.

As we were completing the writing of this manuscript,
Newsweek magazine devoted its cover story to prayer. The
writers reported this same strong tie between prayer and
intimacy, stating that surveys by the sociologist-writer Andrew Greeley "show that spouses who pray together report
greater marital satisfaction than those who don't, and that
frequent sex coupled with frequent prayer make for the
most satisfying marriages."†

One husband we interviewed wrote: "My wife and I consider our sexual intimacy to be an area of prayer. We pray
that each time we make love, we will fall more deeply in

* Collins, *Christian Counseling*, p. 190.
† "Talking to God," *Newsweek* (January 6, 1992) 119:1, p. 41.

our friends been praying together and opening their hearts to God before one another, there would not have been any room for a "stranger" in either of their lives. As one couple told us: "We are each other's spiritual sounding board and counselor."

Daily prayer can serve as the guardian of the marriage, for the husband and wife who pray together do not pray alone. God Himself is present and He will not tolerate any duplicity. He will, on the other hand, encourage the formation of an ever-closer bond and He will lend His strength to that bond so that nothing can break it.

The Orthodox Church in America has, in its Ceremony of Matrimony, a carefully worded litany that points toward intimacy. The Reverend David Ford of St. Tikhon's Seminary in South Canaan, Pennsylvania, shared it with us and we have used it in our prayer time. It is especially appropriate on an anniversary. We have taken the liberty of adapting the wording slightly:

> That You will send down upon us perfect and
> peaceful love, and assistance, we pray to the
> Lord.
> Lord, have mercy.
> That You will preserve us in oneness of mind, and
> in steadfast faith, we pray to the Lord.
> Lord, have mercy.
> That you will preserve us in a blameless way of life,
> we pray to the Lord.
> Lord, have mercy.
> That the Lord our God will grant us an honorable
> marriage and a bed undefiled, we pray to the
> Lord.
> Lord, have mercy.

love. Couples need to pray about sexuality, for it is an area where men and women do not understand each other's needs. It is also a prime cause of divorce."

Intimacy in prayer, then, is found to be a strong ally to intimacy in every other area of the marriage relationship. It is as if Pam and I can hear Dad Rosewell saying, as he did on our wedding day, that marriage can be "the pinnacle of man's delight" if you "get it right." Prayer helps you get it right.

Recovering a Lost Art

Far from being a recent development, husband-wife prayer has been urged by leaders of the Church from the very beginning. With the help of Thomas Oden of Drew University and David Ford of St. Tikhon's Orthodox Seminary, Pam and I learned of two early examples.

One is from the sermons of the great preacher of the late fifth and early sixth centuries, St. John Chrysostom, bishop of Constantinople. In his homily on Ephesians 5:22–33, Chrysostom teaches husbands:

> Whenever you give your wife advice, always begin by telling her how much you love her. . . . Show her that you value her company, and prefer being at home to being out. Esteem her in the presence of your friends and children. Praise and show admiration for her good acts; and if she ever does anything foolish, advise her patiently. Pray together at home and go to Church; when you come back home, let each ask the other the meaning of the readings and the prayers.*

* St. John Chrysostom, *On Marriage and Family,* translated by Catharine P. Roth and David Anderson (Crestwood, N.Y.: St. Vladimir's Seminary Press, 1986), p. 61

The other comes from 200 A.D. and the life of a Roman Christian of North Africa, Tertullian, who left many writings to posterity. One was entitled "To His Wife" and is divided into two parts. In the first, he sought to leave a testament for his wife, whom he called his "best beloved fellow-servant in the Lord." It would serve her well in the event that he died before she. He laid out the virtues of the single life and called her to remain unmarried in the service of Christ. In the second part he wrote "the next best advice," explaining why it would be best for a Christian woman to remain single in widowhood but offering her God's blessing should she choose rather to re-marry. (Actually, Tertullian's wife died first and he remained single until his death.) At the close of this document, Tertullian pays a high tribute to his wife and to the intimate marriage.

> Whence are we to find words enough fully to tell the happiness of that marriage which the Church cements, which angels carry back the news of to heaven, which the Father holds for ratified? What kind of yoke is that of two believers, partakers of one hope, one desire, one discipline, one and the same service? Both are brethren, both fellow servants; there is no difference of spirit or of flesh. Indeed, they are truly "two in one flesh." Where the flesh is one, one is the spirit too. Together they pray, together prostrate themselves, together perform their fasts—mutually teaching, mutually exhorting, mutually sustaining. Equally are they both found in the Church of God; equally at the banquet of God; equally in straits, in persecutions, in refreshments. Neither hides aught from the other; neither shuns the other; neither is troublesome to the other. . . .

Between the two echo psalms and hymns; and they mutually challenge each other which shall better chant to their Lord. Such things when Christ sees and hears, He joys. To these He sends His own peace. Where two are, there is He Himself. Where He is, there the Evil One is not.*

Moved as we are by every line in this portrait of two equal "fellow-servants" who shared all of the good and the bad of life as one, we are struck especially by the phrase, "together they pray." And we marvel at the miracle, still true, that when a husband and wife pray together, "there is He Himself . . . sending His own peace." To those couples who seek to know Him through prayer this is the gracious offer the Lord holds out today.

---

* From "To His Wife" by Tertullian, *The Ante-Nicene Fathers*, vol. IV (Grand Rapids: Eerdmans), p. 48. This excerpt has been modernized and edited slightly.

Carey Moore is serials and reference librarian at Dallas Baptist University. His wife, **Pamela Rosewell Moore,** is an author, conference speaker, and the director of spiritual life at the university.